WILD AND TAME

'Erik Sletholt has an exceptional flair for animals. His powers of observation and enjoyment are remarkable; his touch is sure, and he writes extremely well. But the underlying purpose is serious: he presents a solemn warning about our failure to understand the balance of nature and the senseless brutality with which we continue to exploit and exterminate animals. For those actively concerned with nature his book is a must: it has a message for us all.'

Dr. Olav A. Berg, President of the Norwegian SPCA and Professor of Pathology at the Norwegian Veterinary College, Oslo.

'Erik Sletholt really knows the animals he is writing about ... I particularly admire his attitude towards beasts of prey, which is based on a deep understanding of the interplay of nature ... Because they depend on personal experience, Sletholt's conclusions are likely to receive much more attention than the theories of many academic scientists. This is a book that every animal-lover will benefit from reading.'

Sverre M. Fjelstad (a leading Norwegian authority on wild life) in *Aftenposten*.

WILD AND TAME

a view of animals

Erik Sletholt

Translated from the Norwegian
by Oliver Stallybrass

with line drawings by
Egil Torin Naesheim

CHARLES SCRIBNER'S SONS · NEW YORK

1 3 5 7 9 11 13 15 17 19 I/C 20 18 16 14 12 10 8 6 4 2

Printed in Great Britain
Library of Congress Catalog Card Number 75—24831

ISBN 0-684-14520-0

1891808

CONTENTS

To my wife Ciska, who has given me endless help and support in my animal studies, and who has kept open house for all the curious creatures who over the years have flocked to our door.

PREFACE

Since I was a boy I have always had a strong sense of kinship with nature and the animal world. For much of my life I have enjoyed the rare privilege and happiness of living in close harmony with nature—or what remains of it; and all my most memorable experiences have been with animals.

Most of these experiences occurred in North America, which still contains vast stretches of wilderness where few, if any, white men have set foot. In these areas one can still find nature and animal life in their unspoiled state—although there are signs that even these last outposts will soon yield to the march of civilization.

This book is about some of the wild animals I have come to know, including some who have grown up with our own dogs and cats. It is not a zoology textbook, nor does it have any scientific pretensions. But the incidents described in it are true. The conclusions I have drawn are based on my own experiences, supplemented in some cases by discussions with Indians and white lumberjacks who have spent a lifetime in the wild—and who possess not only an unrivalled knowledge and understanding of animal life, but also the deepest reverence for it.

E.S.

Some years ago I came across a herd of wild horses in their natural environment. It was in a remote valley in a wild and almost inaccessible area at the foot of the Rockies, in the southern part of Alberta, in the late afternoon one day in early summer. I had been in the saddle all day, and my old mare Sally was as tired as I was.

I was chatting away to her when we came to a little clearing in the trees and I suggested we should camp there for the night. Sally responded with a whinny of pleasure, and the matter was settled. I relieved her of the saddle and pack, turned her loose in the lush green meadow, and wandered off in search of firewood. First, however, I wanted to survey the area, so I climbed to the top of a ridge.

Suddenly I found myself overlooking a little subsidiary valley that was new to me; and down there, lo and behold, was a herd of wild horses grazing peacefully on the succulent mountain grass. There were about forty animals in all, evidently feeling quite secure, even in this territory, from grizzly bears and cougars. The reason soon became apparent: quite close to me, on the crest of a hill, stood a magnificent chestnut stallion, his mane streaming out behind him. He was keeping watch until his herd had had its fill.

I didn't wish to disturb them, but I very much wanted to get a closer look; so, as carefully as possible, I crept to a better vantage-point. I don't think the stallion heard or saw me, but he must have caught my scent, because he suddenly raised his head and sniffed the air. Then he gave his warning neigh, and the next moment they were off—in that effortless, flowing gallop that only wild horses can display. It was a picture of colour and grace—one of the loveliest sights I have ever seen.

Fear had scattered the horses: fear of the only natural

enemy they have—man. A grizzly bear or a cougar would have met with a challenge from the assembled herd; but a man was another matter. The scent alone was enough to put these proud, fearless animals to flight.

Later, sitting by my camp fire, I brooded dejectedly over this phenomenon—while Sally tried to console me by rubbing her soft muzzle against my neck. Wherever man sets foot he sows the seeds of suspicion and fear. Only in the remotest areas, hundreds of miles from civilization, do we find animals still living in peace with the world around them. A man who wanders into such a place is regarded with cautious curiosity—not with actual fear or hostility— unless he becomes guilty of a breach of confidence. Today such places are few and far between.

Of course we can talk of fear within the animal kingdom, but this is an altogether different emotion from fear of man. It is an instinctive caution—an alarm-bell rung by the senses against the threat of danger, which causes animals to seek sanctuary as far away as possible. After all, there are species which depend on other species for their survival. The fox, for example, eats woodland birds, hares and field-mice; so it's hardly surprising if these creatures avoid him. Even a roe will take flight when a fox approaches. An elk, on the other hand, won't even lay back his ears—though obliged, on occasion, to take flight before adversaries like the wolf, the cougar and the grizzly. In northern latitudes only these three are without natural enemies in the animal kingdom, man being the only creature that they have learned to fear.

Nature is indeed red in tooth and claw, and in the animal world there is one inflexible rule: only he who can look after himself will survive. Animals know this, and yet they are capable of unparalleled courage in the hour of danger. The sacrifice that an animal will make for her young could well serve as an example to many human beings. A mother hare will go for the fox who is threatening her offspring, though she knows it means certain death; and a pair of titmice will attack the crows who are trying to steal their eggs. But nature once was well adjusted, maintaining a balance between the species—until modern man with his technological progress began to throw everything into confusion and destroy the ecological harmony.

At one time man had to hunt in order to stay alive; but today only a tiny percentage of the earth's population depends for its food on hunting. Yet animal life, including marine life, is as necessary as ever if we are to maintain a balance in nature instead of destroying it, as we are doing now. We have killed most of the wild life around us and are busily polluting the waters of our planet, as well as the soil and atmosphere.

Factories and drains, spewing more and more filth into rivers, inland seas and oceans, have wrought havoc among fish and other marine life. Oil slicks—ever larger and more widespread—each year kill hundreds of thousands of sea-birds, and thousands of seals and other warm-blooded marine animals. The enormous Lake Erie has been declared poisonous and a danger to health. In Europe the Rhine is contaminated to such an extent that the entire Dutch people is in danger, since they get all their fresh water from the river, and its mercury content is well over the safety level. In Egypt, the Aswan Dam has checked the natural flow of the Nile, which is now but a dead vein of water, its course so leisurely that brackish water from the Mediterranean has forced its way many miles upstream and killed off the fish. The river is now full of disease-carrying snails, while thousands of men who used to fish the estuary for their livelihood are back-street beggars in Cairo and Alexandria. In Australia, starfish are eating the coral reefs that protect the coast, their natural enemies having been exterminated by man. Disappearance of the reefs could mean national disaster.

In South America, countries such as Peru and Bolivia have experienced a catastrophe that has caused the worst crisis in their history. Insecticides, mainly DDT, have killed the off-shore plankton and anchovies; and the seabirds that lived off the anchovies can no longer produce the same quantities of the guano on which the agriculture of these countries depends—with the result that food production has fallen far below the critical level.

3

And for all this we have ourselves to thank. In our insane pursuit of material gain we have lost touch with the natural life around us. We no longer understand it, and we fail to realize that the smallest living creature is part of life itself and has its own essential purpose in the world we all share and inhabit.

The Indians in the great plains and forests of North America have learned to live in harmony with nature, and to feel a profound respect for the animal world. We may regard them in many ways as primitive, but they are much wiser than we, and they long ago proved that the only way to live *off* nature is to live *with* nature. Our technology will be of little use to us when our water is poisoned, our atmosphere polluted, and our topsoil incapable of sustaining vegetable life.

We have much to learn from the beasts. If only we can get on to their wavelength we may yet manage to preserve what remains of our natural environment

Anyone who imagines that a fox, or any other wild animal, can fend for himself in the natural state after living all his life with human beings should think again. I know for certain that Hans—a Norwegian red fox of the purest pedigree—could never have managed it.

Many people, of course, have read about the lioness Elsa, who grew up with her human adoptive parents, the Adamsons, and later returned to the wild, found a mate, and produced cubs which she subsequently introduced to her foster-parents. But this proves only that in a single instance, in very special circumstances and with a fantastic share of luck, the experiment succeeded.

Elsa was never completely cut off from her natural milieu. The Adamsons lived in the jungle, surrounded by lions and other wild animals, and Elsa never completely lost touch with her own kin. Nevertheless, she found great difficulty in being accepted by the family she settled with. Indeed, she was very lucky not to be torn to pieces by the other lionesses in the harem. The Adamsons were trying to prove that, granted the necessary goodwill and understanding, it is possible for a much more intimate relationship between men and animals to be established than is normally the case; but the experiment could easily have ended in Elsa's premature death.

Our red fox Hans was a case in point, as the end of this story will show. We had acquired him originally when the hunters who had shot his parents and three of his brothers and sisters suddenly had qualms of conscience and allowed my brother to take home with him the two cubs, one male and one female, that still survived. They were christened Hans and Grethe. Our parents refused to let us keep more than one fox in the house, so Grethe had to find another home. Since my brother lived in Oslo and only came home at the weekend, it was I who became responsible for Hans's upbringing. And Hans, though scarcely two months old, was a handful.

On the very first day in his new home he contrived to create a situation which placed his future in grave jeopardy. The problem was that he led an exceedingly active night-life, which made it almost impossible for the other members of the household to sleep. I had prepared a bed for him in the cellar, but he had no intention of going to sleep, and it wasn't long before he found his way into the larder, where somehow he managed to get in among my mother's preserves, which were her pride and joy.

In the middle of the night we were all woken by a series of explosions from down below. Each member of the family sat up in bed, rubbed his bleary eyes, put on his slippers, and stumbled along the dark corridors and down the cellar stairs. I still shudder when I recall the sight that met our eyes as we trooped into the larder. I am convinced that only my innate powers of persuasion saved Hans from instant death that night.

He had used a table to clamber up on to the bottom shelf. He could only go forward, but the shelf wasn't particularly wide, and the gap between the outer edge and the serried ranks of bottles and jars was too narrow for him to pass. However, there was also a gap at the back, between the rear rank and the wall. This too was a bit narrow, but Hans soon discovered that the bottles and jars stood dutifully aside when he pushed forward between them and the wall. Naturally he chose the easiest route.

The fearful bang that occurred every time a jar hit the ground made him nervous, so he pressed on at full speed. That was why we were woken by what sounded like a slightly retarded burst of machine-gun fire.

Next, I tried to get Hans to sleep in a secluded little cloakroom by my bedroom, in a basket which I had fitted out with a large soft blanket, lent me, as a great favour, by my mother. For the first hour Hans was relatively quiet, being—as I afterwards discovered—busily engaged in tearing the blanket to shreds. When that job was completed to his satisfaction, he turned his attention to my bedroom door; and of course in the end I had to let him in. For the

rest of the night he kept me awake with an uninterrupted series of surprise attacks on my toes.

After several unsuccessful attempts to keep him tethered in a corner of the bedroom, I built a solid cage for him out in the garden. He broke out of it the very first night: his teeth were too strong for the chicken-wire, and I had to rebuild it with tougher material. This did the trick, but during the following nights he occupied himself by giving one-man shows, which consisted in serenading the moon—whether the moon was there or not. From time to time he would interrupt his concert to refill his lungs. Then I would grow nervous, and feel constrained to go out and see whether anything had happened to him, which of course it hadn't. It became fairly clear, however, that Hans had the edge over me in intelligence. The intervals in his serenading evidently attracted my attention—and so, as early as the second night, the intervals became more frequent. I would decline to react immediately; he would wait for a while; then if nothing happened he would produce a series of pitiful whimpers, as if some monster were eating him alive, and I would come.

It all ended, I need hardly say, with a victorious Hans moving back into my bedroom—for good.

To this day I don't know if it is possible to train a fox to sleep during the night instead of the day, but Hans and I finally came to a kind of understanding. He allowed me to fall asleep around midnight; then he would wake me again at about five in the morning. What he did during those five hours I have no idea.

At the time, we were living in the commandant's residence in the disused Seiersten fortress at Drøbak, some twenty miles south of Oslo, with a superb view from the ramparts of the Oslo fjord. The place, which was military property, was surrounded by woods on all sides, and its isolation made it ideal for bringing up animals. Hans was generally free to go where the spirit took him, but from time to time he found himself tied to a string like an ordinary watchdog, and this became an unalterable rule on Sundays, after Hans had let his sense of duty run away with him and landed us in trouble once or twice.

My father's commanding officer made a habit of coming out to Seiersten on Sundays, where he liked to wander around on the ramparts, surveying his military kingdom. Since the ramparts were open to the public, the house and garden were fenced in, and most people followed a path that led past the property on the other side of the fence. But not the colonel. To save time he used our drive, coming and going through a pair of gates on either side of the property. We didn't mind, and in any case it would have been difficult for my father to object if his commanding officer wished to take this liberty. But Hans acknowledged no commanding officer and strongly resented the colonel's intrusion. No outsider was allowed to make free with his private property—and in his view the colonel was an outsider.

While he was still small, Hans contented himself with behaving in a threatening manner whenever the colonel came through the gate, following him like a shadow all the way to the other gate, but maintaining a respectful distance. As he grew older and bigger, however, he grew bolder as well—and one day he launched an attack on the unfortunate man.

Our Sunday meditations were interrupted by loud cries and violent military oaths, and we emerged on to the veranda to find Hans and the colonel engaged in bitter combat. The colonel was kicking and hitting out with his walking-stick, while Hans was jumping nimbly out of range after each of his attempts to bite his adversary's leg. He was immensely pleased with himself—this was clear from his expression—and was very puzzled by our failure to share his enthusiasm.

My poor father was subjected to the direst threats from the enraged colonel, who demanded Hans's immediate death—as a curtain-raiser for the drama to follow. I had a strong impression that he would not be satisfied until he saw me, my father and the entire family hung, drawn and quartered. Fortunately my father was a diplomatic man and, as the colonel cooled down, his plans of revenge were abandoned one by one. Hans wisely changed his tactics, and he and the colonel became the best of friends.

Hans and I went for a long walk in the woods every day, and I was always curious to see what would happen if he met one of the regular inhabitants. One day my curiosity was gratified. Hans was walking in front of me when he suddenly dashed away along a side path. He stopped in front of a small spruce whose drooping branches lay partly on the ground, sniffed around for a moment or two and then wriggled his way in between the branches.

The next moment it was as if a powder keg had exploded under the tree. Out through the brushwood on one side burst an outsize hare, and out through the branches on the other side rushed Hans. They both tore off as if propelled by rockets—but in opposite directions. Within a matter of seconds Hans had disappeared, and my repeated calls had no effect whatsoever. When I finally got home I found Hans under my bed, still in a state of shock, and trembling at the terrible experience he had had out in the wood.

He fared little better on the neighbouring farm where I used to go for eggs and milk. One day I took him with me, confident that he would do no mischief. When we came into the yard, all the poultry were there, and I speculated a little on what Hans's reaction would be; for, believe it or not, he had never seen a hen in his life before. He was almost bursting with curiosity, but at the same time he was uncertain quite how to behave towards these strange new creatures, so at first he kept close to my heels.

I had collected my pail of milk and basket of eggs, and was all set to leave, when we heard a tremendous hullabaloo out in the farmyard. Hans had evidently been unable to contain his curiosity any longer, and since the hens did not appear to be particularly dangerous he had decided to have bit of fun with them. He crept up on a hen with some exceptionally fine tail-feathers, took a grip on the brilliant plumage, and pulled.

The hen cackled and beat her wings dementedly. Hans didn't resist, but neither did he let go. Instead he allowed himself to be dragged at high speed through the flock of hens, who scattered, screeching and flapping in all directions. It was all good clean fun, in Hans's view—until the pasha whose harem it was joined in the game. This was a large, bad-tempered cock, who may have had some previous experience of foxes. At all events, to see one of his hens being tormented by this monster was more than he could bear; and without a moment's hesitation he flew at Hans, beak and spurs flailing. Poor Hans, who had merely been enjoying an innocent game, made off in terror as fast as his legs would carry him. After this I could never get him to come with me into this particular farmyard; he preferred to wait outside the gate while I fetched the milk and eggs.

On the way home we passed a meadow where another farmer grazed his horses and cattle. As soon as we reached the meadow Hans would squeeze under the barbed-wire fence and rush in among the normally peaceful livestock. His presence invariably had the most inflammatory effect: as soon as he appeared the cows would go for him with lowered horns, and it was never long before the horses joined in the pursuit of little Hans. Hans was beside himself for joy as he cavorted like an acrobat between the perilous horns and hooves.

The excitement of the game was such that he took not the slightest notice when I called. Again and again I held my breath as it seemed that Hans was completely surrounded and was bound to end up under the stamping hooves or on the tossing horns. I need not have worried: the large, heavy animals had no chance against the fox's lightning movements and incredible agility. Throughout the performance he seemed to be wearing a sly smile; I almost believe he derived a sadistic pleasure from the sight of his opponents puffing and panting with exertion, while he himself remained as fresh as a daisy.

Hans had an instinctive fear of dogs—a fear which proved well-grounded on more than one occasion. When dogs chased him on his own territory there was no danger, since he knew every useful nook and cranny, and had no difficulty in giving his pursuers the slip. But his occasional trips with me into the town were another matter. He hated the streets, where he felt hemmed in, with danger lurking round every corner. He seemed to know that in these conditions he had no real chance of standing on his own four feet; instead, whenever he met a dog, he would turn abruptly round and jump up into my arms. There he felt perfectly safe against all the perils to which a fox is exposed.

To my sorrow and consternation Hans was an incorrigible thief, whose kleptomania involved me in many embarrassing situations. In the summer my friends and I used to bathe in a bay of the Oslo fjord, and since this involved a good long walk through the wood I always took Hans with me. Down on the shore I kept an eye on him as much as I could, but whenever I went for a swim he would slink around on his own—until I discovered what he was up to. While I was enjoying myself in the water he would be busily laying in supplies against the hard times that he seemed to anticipate for me.

In the course of the summer I received a considerable collection of stolen goods. At first Hans confined himself to negotiable objects such as watches, wallets, pipes, tobacco tins and packets of cigarettes. These he hid in a cache up in the wood, and when I was dressed and ready to go home he would begin running to and fro bringing the stolen goods—one thing at a time. Most of the items had been taken from my friends, so as a rule it wasn't difficult to restore them to their owners.

But on one occasion I returned from a swim to find the entire beach in an uproar. Hans had apparently stolen first the shirt and then the trousers of a man who was sunbathing, and had made off with them to the wood. Now he sat gazing with an innocent air at the confusion he had created. Since more than one witness had seen him in the act, it was no use my proclaiming his innocence, so I gave him a stern lecture and told him to restore the man's clothes. He plainly didn't want to, but eventually he slouched reluctantly off into the wood. He was gone for such a long time that I was afraid he had taken a short cut home. I felt exceedingly ill at ease, and the hostile attitude of Hans's victim was hardly reassuring. Finally, however, Hans returned with the first item, before setting off back to the wood for the second, which was followed by various smaller objects whose loss no one had noticed.

I could put up with his stealing from myself and from my nearest friends, but when he began stealing from strangers

I felt things were going too far. People might think I had put him up to it. So, although I still allowed him to come with me to the beach, from then on I kept him tied up while I was in the water.

When Hans came to us we had no dog—only a large white Angora cat with a tail almost as big and bushy as his own. These two were friends from the first moment, though Hans soon learned to show a deep respect for the cat. They often played together, and when either of them was asleep the other would sneak up and amuse himself with the sleeper's tail. The cat would use his claws on the fox's brush, without ever injuring him. But in the absence of claws Hans used his teeth on the cat's tail—and that was a very different matter. After getting his snout clawed a couple of times he learned to treat the cat's tail with loving care; and the friendship held.

One day I noticed the cat playing with something out in the grass near the garden fence. He was leaping backwards and forwards in a series of lightning attacks on some unidentified creature. At first I thought he had got hold of a rat; then to my horror I realized it was a large adder. If the cat lacked the sense to clear off, things were bound to end badly, and I began looking round for a stick with which to come to his aid.

But before I could do anything, Hans threw himself into the fray, dancing round the adder like a dervish, and dashing in for a quick bite before leaping back every time he had manoeuvred him off balance. Again and again the cycle was repeated, at such a speed that the whole struggle can't have taken more than a few seconds. The adder had no real chance, and by the time I arrived on the scene he was dead, while the allies sat licking each other in mutual congratulation.

Hans's end was a sad one. In the hunting season we had always kept him securely tethered. But one day, a cousin of ours dropped in on his way to a hunt. In an act of thoughtless folly, he let off his rifle just behind the unsuspecting fox. The unfamiliar noise scared Hans half out of his wits. With a snap of his jaws he bit through his lead and was off into the woods.

I ran after him, but it was quite impossible to catch up with him, or to find his trail in the thick undergrowth, and I very soon gave up the chase. Hans often went exploring in the woods on his own, but he was never away for long, and I reckoned that once the fright had worn off he would return home.

But the hours went by, and there was still no sign of Hans. Later in the afternoon I went back to the wood and searched all night. In vain: Hans had gone, and Hans did not return.

The next day an official came to our house with Hans's collar. He wanted to know what to do with the body. It appeared that Hans had been shot by a friend of ours who was out hunting, and who had been near the house when Hans had disappeared. The man had been standing in a clearing, when a fox had popped out of the wood and come running straight towards him. Almost without thinking, he had raised his rifle and fired at point blank range.

The man had been half aware that there was something odd about the situation, but the whole thing had happened too quickly, and it was only when he bent over the dead fox that he discovered the collar round his neck. Then it dawned on him that it was his old friend Hans, who had come running to him for protection. And how in the world was Hans to know that in men's eyes all foxes look alike? The man had taken the tragedy so much to heart that he had brought the dead body to the official and asked him to break the news to us. It was small consolation that Hans's death had been quick and relatively painless.

After my experience with Hans I became convinced that one should never take a wild animal out of his natural environment unless one can guarantee him absolute protection at all times. The worst thing of all is to bring up an animal in captivity and then release him when he is fully grown. Such an animal will seldom survive for long in the wild, for he lacks all the natural skills he needs to survive.

A young animal is like a child. He is born with certain instincts, but these need to be developed by experience. Moreover, the young animal, like the human child, needs to learn many things if he is to stand on his own feet; and the only teachers he has are his parents. In particular it is the mother who teaches her young what they can eat and what they must not touch. She instructs them in the fine points of hunting: how to creep up on their quarry, how to kill it, which species are their natural prey, and—not least—which species they must avoid. These skills are not acquired in a moment: they need time and practice. A young animal growing up without this training is completely helpless. All the instincts in the world cannot replace what only the mother can teach.

Hans lacked this training. After his first encounter with the hare and the neighbour's poultry, he made great detours whenever a hare or grouse was in the offing. Yet these are a fox's natural prey. Conversely, because he had grown up among human beings, he regarded every human being as a friend. His mother would have taught him that man is his deadliest enemy, whom he should keep at the greatest possible distance. And so Hans died in his prime, because he had never had a mother to teach him an important lesson.

THREE   NAMU, THE KILLER WHALE

Nobody, as far as I am aware, has ever been privileged to study a killer whale in its natural environment. There are, of course, hundreds of seafaring men who have observed these animals out in the ocean, but such observations have all been of very limited duration, made under special circumstances.

My own experience is no exception. But I did once have the opportunity of making some fairly exhaustive studies of a killer whale in captivity—the first such to survive for more than a few days. And, although my observations are not necessarily valid for killer whales in general, they seem to be largely borne out by reports on others of the species captured subsequently and still alive.

The killer whale I studied was called Namu, and became world-famous after starring as himself in a film of that title.

Apart from a few stuffed museum specimens, and fleeting glimpses of a school of four or five of them during one of my voyages, I had never before seen a killer whale at close quarters when I first encountered Namu near Seattle in March 1966. I was at once deeply impressed, both by the immense streamlined body with its beautiful silky skin, black above and cream below, and by Namu's obvious intelligence and friendly good nature.

The killer whale, or—to use the scientific name— *Orcinus orca*, is the largest and most intelligent of the Delphinidae family, within the sub-order of Odontoceti or toothed whales. (Namu, who was not full-grown, was about twenty-six feet long and weighed six tons. His powerful dorsal fin, consisting entirely of muscle, was about six feet long.) The killer whale has been an object of dread since the dawn of time, and he owes his name to the belief that (apart from man) he is the only warm-blooded animal that kills for 'sport'. The man-eating shark, so legend goes, is an innocent in comparison with the blood-thirsty *Orcinus orca*.

16

Travellers' tales from the fishing fleets of the world are full of grisly details about the killer whale: that he tears men to pieces and gobbles them up, or that he bites out and swallows the tongues of the large whales—for fun. These reports may well be true, though the motive can hardly be the one suggested. In general, however, the killer whale's staple diet is a mixture of fish, cuttlefish and seal.

Everything said and written until now about *Orcinus orca* has been based on rumour, guesswork and sudden unexpected collisions between him and man. Nobody was able to study him quietly at close quarters until June 1965, when a young male swam into a little bay on the west coast of Canada to rescue a still younger animal that had got caught in a salmon-net. When the fishermen realized what had happened, they paid out two more nets in honour of their traditional enemy. It ended with the youngster escaping, and the would-be rescuer becoming hopelessly entangled. This was Namu, so called after the British Columbian fishing-village where he was captured.

On his arrival at Seattle, after a highly publicized journey down the coast, Namu drew bigger crowds than the Beatles, who were there at the same time.

Namu exercised himself every day with his owner, Ted Griffin, whom he allowed to sit astride his back and cling to his immense dorsal fin, while he swam at tremendous speed round and round the large isolated bay that he had to himself. Later, to please the film people, Namu swam round the bay on his back supporting on his belly a sixteen-foot motorboat with three apprehensive actors on board. Namu hardly lived up to his reputation as a devil of the sea, but perhaps he was a special case.

Orcinus orca is one of several species of dolphin which, like the elephant, has a brain larger than man's. Certainly Namu convinced me of the killer whale's high level of intelligence. His perceptiveness and grasp of situations were astonishing. For example, when he swam around with the motorboat on his belly, he knew perfectly well that it would capsize unless it was propped up—so he held it firmly in position with his flippers, one on each side. He knew his own enormous strength, and was always very

17

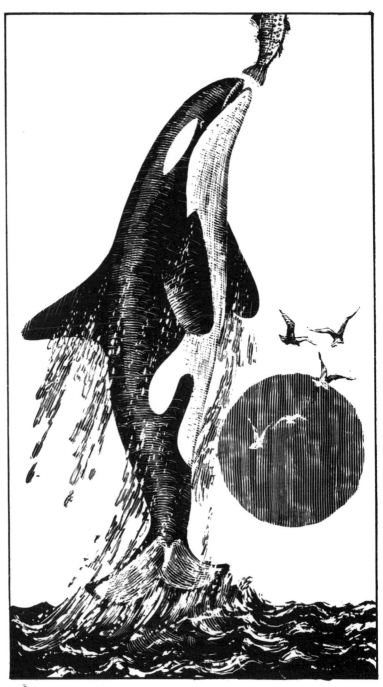

careful not to injure his human friends when playing with them in the water.

Killer whales usually live in schools. Namu, cut off from his own kind, turned to human beings for the company and affection that he needed in large quantities. He liked to have someone to talk to, and to have his belly scratched and his snout patted at regular intervals. He was immensely patient, and good-humoured even when teased. According to Griffin he did occasionally grow angry, but he never did more than turn his back and swim off to a corner of his bay, where he could remain undisturbed.

I have seen Namu shoot out of the water ten or twelve feet into the air. Think of the strength needed to get six tons up to that height. One experiment we often tried consisted of holding a morsel of salmon—his favourite food—just above the surface of the water. When Namu stuck his head out of the water to take the salmon, the man holding it would gradually lift it higher and higher. Namu would follow at exactly the same speed, until he was as far out of the water as he could get without actually taking off. Then he would sink back gently and wait. This performance might be repeated two or three times, and Namu would bear it all with great patience. He could so easily have sprung up, and taken fish, hand and man at one gulp; but that never seemed to occur to him. When at last he was given his morsel of fish, he would take it carefully between his great teeth without even touching the hand that held it.

While he lived, Namu was the subject of intensive research by the American navy and air force. The navy was particularly interested in his built-in sonar—a kind of under-water radar. Namu had good eyesight, but when he was on the move he relied entirely on his sonar, which enabled him to discover and identify everything in the water for great distances around him. This system works by the emission of sound waves through the skin. When the waves meet resistance in the water, they are reflected and supply information on the precise nature and location of the resistance.

All Delphinidae, of course, have this sonar device. One experiment, conducted with a common dolphin, consisted of marking out a kind of slalom course of iron stakes in his pool, and then blindfolding and releasing him. The dolphin covered the entire course at speed, without hitting any of the numerous stakes.

The Delphinidae's use of sonar to establish the presence of a fish in their vicinity has been scientifically proved, but their apparent ability to identify the *kind* of fish remains a mystery. An experiment we tried on Namu produced some astonishing results. He didn't always choose to come when called, but he could never resist salmon; and whenever we smacked the water with a piece of salmon he would come hurtling like a torpedo from the other side of the bay. We tried to fool him with a tasty piece of cod fillet, but it was a waste of time—he refused to budge. Then we changed the bait to salmon again, and within seconds he was there to claim his titbit. We repeated this experiment time after time, and it never failed. He lived almost entirely on salmon— two hundred pounds a day! Sometimes he would make do with other fish, cuttlefish, seal or sea birds, but only if salmon was totally unobtainable. This predilection is no doubt the reason why the killer whale is regarded as Public Enemy Number One by the fishermen of the west coast of Canada.

I have said that Namu liked to talk to his friends. That is an understatement—he was positively garrulous. During the year he lived in captivity, all his chatter and all his conversations with his friends outside his own bay were tape-recorded. It is now clear beyond doubt that killer whales communicate in their own language. Above surface level they emit sounds through their blowholes, but under water, as we have seen, they send out sound waves through their skin. Most of these sounds can be picked up by the human ear, but some of the sound waves have such high frequencies that they are inaudible to us, though they can be recorded by special apparatus.

Namu was visited several times by members of his own species, who came up to the net which barred access to his bay. On these occasions Namu would swim over to them and talk for a while, after which they would go their separate ways. It was always easy to tell whether his visitor was a male or a female: if it was a male, Namu would talk in his normal tone, but if it was a female his voice would shoot up several octaves, and he would speak much more rapidly.

Griffin used a wire cage to float Namu down to Seattle from the Canadian fishing village. It was open at the top, and was drawn by a fishing smack with the aid of cables. *En route* they met a large school of killer whales, possibly the very school that Namu had once belonged to. On discovering the prisoner the whales at once attacked both the boat and the cage, apparently with the object of liberating their kinsman. The crew were not particularly alarmed for their own safety, but there was no doubt that the school was perfectly capable of tearing the cage to ribbons and releasing their expensive prisoner.

But then Namu began talking to them—loudly and clearly. They immediately abandoned their attack, and after a long conference drew away from the cage and allowed the boat to continue. It was almost as if Namu had assured them that everything was in order and that he had suffered no injury or inconvenience. Nevertheless, the school remained for a long time in the neighbourhood, and every now and then they would come up and talk to Namu in his cage.

When we spoke to Namu he invariably answered. What he said is still beyond the experts' powers of interpretation; but the day may come when someone discovers the key to killer-whale language. Griffin spent many hours listening to the tapes, and learned to imitate many of Namu's sounds. This enabled him to have numerous 'conversations' with Namu—though he hadn't the remotest idea what they were all about, and Namu probably regarded him as a hopeless dunce.

Personally I cannot help feeling that Namu was much more than 'just an animal', and that he had a very distinct personality, with feelings and reactions very similar to those of a human being. When he had hurt himself or was depressed for some reason or other, he would talk in a whining voice, almost like a whimpering child. If he was happy and contented, his voice took on a chirping tone reminiscent of certain kinds of birdsong. If he was in a bad mood, he would give out a deep croaking sound not unlike a frog, or low like a calf. We never knew what he was trying to say, but his feelings were unmistakable.

It was Ivan Tors, the man who owns the dolphin 'Flipper' and has made many films about him, who decided to make a film about Namu. Four Hollywood stars were engaged to act alongside Namu, and the director chosen was Laslo Benedek.

It was decided that the film should be an accurate account of Namu's life from the day he was captured until the day he regained his freedom. The only changes to the plot were in the opening sequence—with the aim of making the whole story more romantic—and in the final scene, where Namu wins his freedom. This had not yet happened; but of course the film had to have a 'happy ending'.

The film was excellent, with some splendid performances from the actors—not least from Namu. Namu repeats the manoeuvre that was carried out the first time Griffin rowed out to him in the bay, except that in the film it is Robert Lansing who sits at the oars. Namu comes up to the boat from below and begins playing water polo with it—always taking care, however, not to destroy or capsize it. All this was absolutely in accordance with what had happened. Griffin had begun by feeding Namu from his little boat, but when Namu found an endless supply of salmon emanating from the boat, he concluded that it must be full of it. Evidently he decided that one piece at a time was too slow, and finally overturned the boat so as to get his dinner served in one magnificent helping. After that, Griffin was obliged to bring the daily ration to the little jetty at the head of the bay.

The world's largest scrubbing-brush was also kept on this little jetty. It was three-feet long, not including the handle, and was used regularly for scrubbing Namu's belly and back—something he regarded as a special treat.

Orcinus orca is beyond comparison the animal world's fastest mover in the water. Nobody has yet succeeded in timing his top speed, but estimates place it at between thirty and forty miles an hour. The reason why no definite figure has been established is simply that no one has succeeded in explaining to a killer whale the object of the exercise, that he shall swim in a straight line for a specified distance as fast as he can. He swims in his own way—he zigzags, he dives, he leaps out of the water, he alternately dawdles and sprints. Time means nothing to him.

But I did once time Namu doing about thirty miles an hour. He was lying peacefully at the far end of the bay when we lured him to the jetty with a fresh salmon. The relatively short distance was covered in what seemed the twinkling of an eye; yet even so he was not moving as fast as I have seen him move on other occasions, and I am inclined to believe that his maximum speed is more like forty.

Namu never tried to escape from captivity. He could easily have jumped over the fishing-net that confined him to his bay, or used his enormous strength to force his way through, but he never attempted either. One theory is that his sonar waves bounced back off the net, that in consequence he had no idea what lay beyond it, and that he was too cautious to risk finding out. My objection to this theory is that he was constantly receiving visits from his relatives beyond the net, and that their presence alone, not to mention what they doubtless told him, would have been sufficient proof that all was well on the other side. Yet he never tried to accompany them when they left at the end of their visit. He had simply turned towards men—and he liked their company.

Griffin felt it was wrong for Namu to live completely cut off from his own kind, and he and his assistant tried hard to find a mate for him, but without success. They did in fact capture a female killer whale, but only a young one, whom they sent down the coast to grow up in the Marineland of the Pacific at San Diego. She was christened Shamu, and is still at San Diego. She has long since been joined by other killer whales, who also seem to thrive in their new life.

When Namu died, about six weeks before the film's world première in Seattle, the whole city was plunged in mourning. The tragic circumstances were as follows. Like all warm-blooded animals the killer whale has a rutting season, and during one of these a female began swimming around just outside the net guarding Namu's bay. Namu went wild with desire. Until now he had found human company more than adequate, but with this enchanting creature just outside his front door he could no longer resist temptation: he had to get out. But for some reason or other, instead of jumping the net or breaking through it, he chose to go underneath. The net was fastened to the bottom by solid steel cables, and it was these that proved Namu's undoing. He wrenched the net free from the bottom and passed beneath it, but his dorsal fin got caught between two cables, and he could move neither forwards nor backwards.

A killer whale, like other Delphinidae, cannot stay under water indefinitely: he has to come up for air. Normally the Dolphin family surface at least once a minute, and the maximum period they can remain under water is a little over twelve minutes. Namu's supply of oxygen gave out before he could break loose from the cables, and he drowned.

During his year in captivity Namu destroyed a multitude of hoary legends about sea monsters. He provided scientists with much valuable information, and taught us a number of salutary truths—if we are wise enough to profit from them. Ivan Tors once said that if we can learn to communicate with animals there is still hope that we may one day learn to communicate with one another. Laslo Benedek's comment was: 'The moment any conflict arises, political, emotional or whatever, we seem to lose the ability to communicate. Whereas it is always possible to communicate with Namu— a "killer whale" such as men have never regarded as other than an enemy.'

And Benedek is right. Namu was always ready to find a peaceful solution to his problems with human beings. But then Namu was wiser than most of us.

It is many years since the Americans abandoned commercial whaling, but in southern California they have recently taken up whale-hunting as a sport—using telescopes, binoculars and cameras. Their quarry is the Californian grey whale, one of the largest in the entire family.

For several winters—with the ready assistance of the Scripps Institution, America's biggest and most important oceanography establishment, with its principal station on the Pacific coast between Los Angeles and San Diego—I had the opportunity of studying the grey whale intensively and at close quarters. From this I learnt a certain amount, but there are still many things about this peaceable, good-humoured giant that I find quite incomprehensible.

At the beginning of December the grey whales begin the long trek southwards from their natural habitat in the Arctic Ocean. Their goal is a 'maternity hospital' more than six thousand miles away: Scammon Lagoon on the west coast of the long Mexican peninsula known as Lower California. This migration, one of the most mysterious and dramatic phenomena in the whole of nature, takes place at exactly same time every year. The route is through the Baring Strait and down the Pacific coast. The greater part of the journey takes place far out at sea, but as they approach their goal the whales come steadily nearer the coast until, by the time they reach the southern part of California, they are very close indeed. Some even enter the skerries, and may at times be seen from the mainland. The vanguard appears in about the middle of January, after which they follow, day after day, in schools of two to fourteen, until the end of February. As the last reach Scammon Lagoon, the first are already homeward-bound with their newborn calves.

This migration of whales has gone on for hundreds of years. It is an unforgettable sight to see whole schools of these gigantic creatures frolicking in the water—diving to the bottom, coming up for air and spouting fifteen-foot vapour jets through their blowholes. The largest ones can measure up to about eighty-five feet and weigh well over forty tons.

The northern Pacific was once full of grey whales—at a rough estimate, somewhere between three hundred thousand and half a million—but that was before the whalers arrived on the scene. As soon as they became aware of the annual migration southwards in January and February, and northwards again in March and April, whaling stations were set up along the entire Pacific coast of North America. From these stations thousands of grey whales were hunted down and killed every year, for oil, meat, bone meal and other products commanding high prices on the world market. It was not long before the stock of grey whales had dwindled to a point where they seemed to be in danger of complete extermination. And when, for a time, the annual migration ceased completely, it was believed that the grey whale had gone the way of the mammoth and the dodo.

But some three hundred to five hundred animals had survived; and to secure the species against extermination an international agreement in 1937 gave the grey whale unconditional protection. The whales resumed migration, as if they knew they no longer had anything to fear, and their numbers have risen to over six thousand—not including those that migrate by another route, down the eastern seaboard of Asia.

In southern California every harbour worthy of the name now has its whaling station; but, as I mentioned above, the hunting based on these is today a peaceful business. Accidents do occur: some whales come too near land and run aground in shallow water; others get entangled in fishing-nets and drown if they are not rescued in time; and one unfortunate creature lost his life after colliding with a naval destroyer. The coastguards do their best to help any that get into difficulties. Frogmen and crane barges are constantly used to release whales caught in the shallows, and I have often seen frogmen straddling the great beasts as they guide them back into deep water.

27

Most of the calves are born in the warm muddy waters of Scammon Lagoon and other smaller lagoons in Lower California. But some cows make the southward journey too slowly and fail to reach the 'maternity hospital' in time. They are then obliged to take shelter anywhere along the coast where they can find a peaceful, well-protected bay, and there they give birth to their calves.

The baby whale is not much less imposing than his parents: he may measure up to sixteen feet at birth, and weigh over fifteen hundredweight. As a warm-blooded mammal, he is entirely dependent on his mother, and is fed with her milk during the first months of his life. His method of feeding is something unique in nature. Whether it was the whale who inspired the modern technique whereby aeroplanes refuel in mid-flight I do not know, but the method is similar. The calf begins by surfacing and filling his lungs with air. Then he dives down under his mother, rolling round on his back, and placing his mouth over one of the slits covering the nipples. This 'fuelling' takes no more than a few seconds, during which special muscles in the mother's body come into action and pump gallons of milk down the baby's throat. Since the baby puts on about two hundredweight a day during the first few weeks of his life, the method is clearly effective.

About a month after the baby is born, he and his parents begin the return journey north. This is the most dangerous stage, and the school stays much farther out to sea. Today they have little to fear from man, but other dangers remain. The young calf is completely defenceless, and the school is haunted by the sea's most dreaded hunter—the killer whale —and to some extent by the larger sharks.

It is the mother's job to protect her calf. In general she is well able to perform this task: her immense size, her speed and her strength make her a formidable adversary against allcomers, and like all animals she will fight for her young with a wild and fearless fury. More than once, her eagerness to protect her calf has led her to attack a perfectly innocent fishing vessel that happened to cross her path. Not long ago a boat full of camera enthusiasts was attacked by an angry mother whale and damaged so severely that it ran aground.

Tragedies often occur during the first days of the journey north. High seas and powerful currents can drive the youngster off course, so that he finishes up on a sandbank or sunken rock. As long as he is under water there is no problem, because sooner or later his mother will find him. But if his body is lying wholly or partly on dry land it is another matter. In the water, the mother's calls and the calf's replies are transmitted as sound waves. But once the calf's body is out of the water, neither set of signals can be received. The mother will swim around for a day or two searching, but unless she finds her offspring by pure chance she will give up and rejoin the school. By then she knows instinctively that he has died.

During one of my cruises in a Scripps Institution boat we found one of these baby whales that had been stranded on a reef just as the tide was beginning to ebb. He had been lying there for at least a day, and there was no sign of his mother. He was still alive, however, and the scientists began working feverishly to save his life. He had been horribly burnt by the sun, and the first essential was to treat the scorched skin with healing ointments. The next was to prepare an enormous bowl of a fluid consisting of dried milk, fish oil, proteins and vitamin preparations. This fluid, the nearest possible equivalent to his mother's milk, was then pumped down the baby's throat by means of a hose. After everything humanly possible had been done to help him, he was placed in an outsize string bag and lowered into the sea, alongside the boat, with his blowhole sticking up out of the water. Now only nature could do the rest—and on this occasion nature failed. The baby whale had been too badly dehydrated, and during the following night he died.

I have been out in a boat many a time to see the winter migration south. It is a lively sight, especially when a male comes shooting up from the depths and hurls his entire mighty body out of the water—whether from sheer exuberance, or to impress the expectant mother, or as a warning to young gallants who have been paying his wife too much attention. On the journey north the whales are no longer so active—they are beginning to grow hungry, and they have to conserve their strength for the long homeward trail.

What is the reason for this remarkable migration—over six thousand miles each way? The answer is simple. Grey whales live on plankton, those microscopic forms of plant and animal life that are found in marine waters. The only place where plankton is sufficiently abundant to support them is the ice-cold waters of the Arctic Ocean. There the grey whale 'pastures' all the summer, gathering strength for the long, hard winter. For as soon as winter begins to descend on the Arctic, and the ice to form, the grey whale—who, of course, has to come up for air at least once in ten minutes—is forced farther and farther south. In addition, the babies will be born some time in February or March. And they need warmer water, where they can gradually build up the layers of fat needed to protect them against the low temperatures of the Arctic waters. So finally, in December, there begins the long trek south to the waters, poor in plankton though they are, of southern California and Mexico.

That—and the grey whales' apparent understanding that they no longer have anything to fear from man—is why we are now able to study them at much closer quarters. And one is grateful for the knowledge that at least this branch of the world's biggest mammal family has, for the time being, been saved from extermination.

The coal-black, two-year-old stallion was silhouetted like a statue against the sky as he stood on the hilltop and gazed out over the rolling country that is so typical of the Rocky Mountain House area of Alberta. Huddled together in a little valley below stood a small herd of mares and foals. Their stamping, and their nervous, muffled neighing, expressed a fear bordering on panic. Only about thirty animals survived of the great herd that had once roamed the plateaux freely and fearlessly. Now they were lean, nervous and too exhausted to benefit from the fresh green grass.

They were in flight, pursued by unfeeling, bloodthirsty hunters armed with the best and most up-to-date equipment. Their original leader, a great, proud stallion, had been killed, as had the wily old mare who had succeeded him. Invincible in his protective instinct, the stallion had urged on his exhausted charges—before turning round for a counter-attack against his pursuers. He had offered an easy target to a large-calibre rifle equipped with telescopic sights, and fired at a safe distance of over a hundred yards.

Usually, when the leader is killed, it is an easy matter to round up and capture the rest of the herd, or at any rate the mares and foals. But not this time. After the death of the old stallion, the survivors had unexpectedly rallied, first round the mare, and later, after her death, round her colt. For three weeks they had fled from hunters who began every day with fresh horses. The young stallion led his little troop so skilfully that for a long time it looked as if he were going to outmanoeuvre his tormentors.

But now fate caught up with him. A shot from a rifle with telescopic sights had brought him down. But he was not dead—not yet. Somehow or other he was up and away, and he recovered so well that he survived the harsh northern winter. He was alone now. But he was still alive when the wild ducks on their way north announced that spring had come. And he was still alive when the summer sun gradually turned the mountain grass from green to brown. But when the days started to draw in and the leaves began to fall, the hunters returned—and the young stallion was on the run once more.

He ran until he nearly collapsed with exhaustion. But he no longer had quite the fire that had saved him earlier. The hunters managed to drive him into an enclosure. He fought for his life when they threw the lasso round his neck, and again when they pushed and pulled him on to the lorry. At Calgary he fought his last, hopeless battle against his human tormentors, and it took over half an hour before the well-trained team got him into the narrow corridor that leads implacably to the slaughterhouse and death.

The wild horses of North America are hunted with snow-scooters in winter, and with jeeps, aeroplanes and helicopters in summer, or with relays of riders on fresh horses. They are shot whenever a hunter catches sight of one, whether he can do anything with the body or not. There are men who regard it as first-rate sport to use a herd of wild horses for target practice—making bets on who can hit most animals, which are then left to die a slow and painful death.

Many wild horses are captured by hunters who sell them for slaughtering; the meat is used as dog-food or as fodder for the great fur farms. A single horse can fetch from fifty to seventy-five dollars if it is large and healthy. The methods of capture and transportation to the slaughterhouse are about as brutal as it is possible to imagine. It is quite common for a horse to arrive with broken legs, bloody sores, and a body riddled with buckshot.

The wild horses are the hippies of the equine world: unshod, unkempt and dishevelled. Some of them stem from generations of wild horses, others were tame until they strayed from the farm where they were born. But all of them are descended from tame animals, from the horses which Cortés and his fellow conquistadors brought to North America in the sixteenth century. The theory has been advanced that there were wild horses in America before the

Spaniards, and although I believe this to be true there is as yet little supporting evidence.

During the last century the buffalo was almost exterminated in North America by a process of senseless slaughter. Now the wild horse is going the same way and will soon be extinct unless the people of the United States and Canada ensure that he is protected. At the turn of the century the two countries contained some three million wild horses; today there are about three thousand in western Canada, and about the same number in the north-western states of the USA.

In Alberta there are three main areas housing a total of about two thousand horses. These areas are not used by farmers or cattle-breeders or for any other purpose. Yet the hunting of the horses continues, with the government's blessing. Every autumn hundreds of animals are captured and despatched to the dog-food factories. This doesn't include all the horses brought down by snipers, or captured by horse-dealers and sold to the big rodeo organizations.

In British Columbia, where there are still more than a thousand wild horses, it is now illegal to shoot or capture them. But this does not eliminate the sniping, much of it done by organized groups.

Why do men have to kill these harmless animals? The answers given are as numerous as they are invalid, a favourite one being that the wild horses eat up fodder needed by domestic horses and cattle. This is plainly absurd: in the areas inhabited by wild horses there are no domestic animals. It is also said that in winter wild horses break down fences in order to help themselves to fodder put out for the domestic animals. In certain cases this may be true, but much more commonly the damage is done by *tame* horses. What happens all too often is that the less scrupulous owners of horses turn them loose in winter to fend for themselves, instead of providing them with hay. These animals normally team up with the wild horses, but as soon as they are hungry they instinctively return to where they know there is food, destroying any fences that obstruct them.

The worst offenders are the great dude ranches—holiday camps that specialize in horseriding. As soon as the season is over, the horses are driven into the forest to fend for themselves; those who survive the winter are rounded up again in the spring. The owners are only interested in making money, and are too mean to feed the horses during the winter.

Wild horses have only one natural enemy: man—whom they have learned to fear above all else. They are extremely shy and wary, taking flight the moment they scent a human presence, and for this reason they are not often seen. But all their caution counts for nothing against the resources of modern technology: swift legs have little chance against helicopters and long-range rifles. The wild horse's day is drawing to an end. **1891808**

There is another proud and beautiful creature which is vanishing from North America. To be sure, there are still plenty of specimens, but as a free-roaming animal it is heading for extinction. I refer to the elk family, two of whose members have already been exterminated, while a third seems doomed—or likely, at best, to survive only as an exhibit in various zoos.

This species, the tule elk, is the smallest in North America, and is popularly known as the dwarf elk. In recent years it has been on the verge of extinction, and in the whole of North America there are not more than about four hundred surviving specimens. As long ago as 1933 there were fears that the species would die out; but then a nature-lover, who happened also to be rich, came to the rescue. He financed the leasing of nearly five hundred square miles in Owens Valley, California, and brought there, on an experimental basis, twenty-six animals from Yellowstone National Park. Over the years the stock grew to about four hundred—the same figure as in 1933.

But that was the limit of growth, because as the numbers increased the neighbouring ranch-owners began complaining that the elk were using up or destroying valuable pastureland. The government gave way to pressure and authorized an extensive slaughter. It was then decided that the stock should be limited to two hundred and fifty to three hundred animals—enough to prevent them from dying out, but not enough to do any damage to pastureland. Whenever it is considered necessary, a massive hunt is organized, and from seventy-five to a hundred animals are shot. Applications to take part in the hunt are dealt with in order of priority, and the result is often a barbaric blood-bath; on one occasion a woman hunter pumped nine bullets into an animal without killing it.

The same problem occurs in the Banff National Park in the Canadian Rockies, where at one point the entire elk population was exterminated. A new parent stock was then success-fully imported from the United States, and the animals multiplied. The balance was maintained by nature herself, and wolves and other beasts of prey kept down the numbers of elk, helped by an occasional epidemic. But then it was decided that the wolves had no useful purpose, and they in turn were exterminated. In consequence the government is now faced with the problem of over-population within the park, where shooting is forbidden. The animals cannot be allowed to starve to death for shortage of pasture, nor can an epidemic be risked any longer—it might wipe out the entire stock. So every autumn sees a slaughter of about two hundred animals to maintain the balance. At least the shooting is done by park-keepers who know how to handle a rifle.

When I suggested to the park authorities that there must be a better solution to the problem than shooting the animals, I received little sympathy. My proposal was to transport small groups of animals in cattle-trucks to some of the numerous areas near the park where elk had previ-ously been exterminated, and which were eminently suited to support them again. I was told that this would be more expensive than shooting them, and they could not afford it.

Fact or flippancy? But in any case what did an animal's life ever mean when money was at stake?

The path I was following through the dense undergrowth was not a path in the normal sense—it was a track worn by animals—but I knew that it would take me to the water I was looking for. I was all alone in the wilds of northern Ontario, far from human habitation. The only people living there were a group of Ojibwa Indians, with whom I had stayed throughout the summer. Instead of allowing themselves to be cooped up in a reserve, like most of the Indian tribes, the Ojibwas had chosen to live in the freedom of an almost inaccessible wilderness, maintaining the traditions of their forebears as hunters and fishermen.

As I ambled along the animals' track, bucket in hand, I had the sense of being followed. I had no idea how long it had gone on, since I lack the instincts that the Indians are born with. But suddenly I was aware of eyes watching me, even though I could hear nothing. I was certain there was no one about, so it must be some kind of animal that was trailing me.

I slowed down a little, and pricked my ears, until my feeling was confirmed beyond all possible doubt by tiny movements in the bushes behind me that had nothing to do with the wind—noises that in normal circumstances I would not have noticed.

Suddenly I turned round. Nothing. Slowly I retraced my steps, carefully studying the footmarks as I went—and then I discovered fresh wolf tracks: it was not a single wolf that had been shadowing me, but a pack of at least four or five. Reassured, I continued down the path to the stream which I could hear ahead of me: I knew now who my travelling companions were, and that I had nothing to fear.

After filling my bucket, I sat down on a tree-stump in a small clearing in the forest for a smoke before setting out again for my camp-site, and on a sudden impulse I decided to try out a few words of the 'wolf language' that the

Ojibwas had taught me. Carefully and not too loudly I gave their call—a yelping sound that ends in a protracted, mournful howl.

The first howl had no immediate effect, though I have to admit that my imitation may not have been quite perfect. However, I tried again, and this time I got a response. Straight in front of me a head appeared out of the bushes. I looked all round, and gradually, one after another, the wolves emerged from the undergrowth. They were five beautiful big specimens of the forest wolf—a little smaller perhaps than the grey wolf that is found in northern parts of Canada and Europe, but with a finer coat. Two of them sat down like great dogs, while the others wandered slowly back and forth. They all observed me carefully, and although they were wary they showed no sign of fear. They may have understood that I was unarmed, or possibly they knew by instinct that I had no evil intentions.

For perhaps ten minutes we sat exchanging thoughts, and then, as if by mutual agreement, they all withdrew and were swallowed up by undergrowth. I in turn picked up my bucket of water and strolled contentedly back to camp.

This is only one of my experiences with the dreaded wolf. For years, off and on, I have lived in wolf territory—there were packs all round our little ranch in western Canada— yet they never attacked any of our domestic animals, or behaved threateningly towards me. There was enough wild life in the area to make it unnecessary for them to hunt domestic animals. The wolf is a cautious animal, and it was not often that one appeared, but I used to see their tracks around our property almost every day.

The wolf has been called a bloodthirsty psychopath and a treacherous coward who only dares attack in large numbers. Never, perhaps, has a fellow creature been so maligned in the popular imagination. There is no fear in the wolf, and as for his wary attitude towards man—that is a sign of intelligence, not cowardice. Like all wild animals he regards the human race with instinctive mistrust, and keeps his distance.

There is a well-known theory that packs of wolves will attack people. I am not going to claim that this has never

happened, but I do not know of a single proven case. It is true that in former times wolves used to attack travellers in the Russian steppes. But this happened in winters when food was scarce and the wolf population was inordinately large. And even then it was not man that the wolves were after, but the horses.

It has been claimed that a pack of wolves will tear apart and devour one of their own kind who has been injured. Again, though I have yet to see the assertion proved, I am prepared to admit the possibility of its being true. But in that case 'bloodthirsty' is a wildly erroneous term. There are, in point of fact, numerous species that kill their sick and injured companions when it is clear that they are going to die in any case, possibly after much suffering. This might be described as nature's own harsh formula for euthanasia. I remember seeing one Christmas on my own veranda a swarm of titmice attack a sick comrade and peck him to death.

There are few warm-blooded animals more intelligent than the wolf; and he is proud and impossible to subdue. He is the only member of the dog family who stubbornly refuses to let himself be deprived of his freedom. He can, of course, be captured and put in a cage, but he can never be tamed, and his will can never be broken. Look at the wolf in his cage in a zoo. He doesn't stand hanging his head like so many of the other unhappy captive animals—he paces up and down, hour after hour, day in, day out, until he dies. And all the time he is searching for a means of escape, hoping for a chance to get out and make his way back to the wild.

Wolves usually hunt in packs, occasionally in pairs, and very seldom alone. There are good reasons for this collaboration. The wolf knows very well that he can never overtake a roe deer, or keep pace with a bull moose. Except for the greyhound there is no swifter member of the dog family, and he can keep trotting at an even pace for hours on end—but he can never overtake large hoofed animals of the antelope species. That is why the wolf needs cunning as well as speed if he is to bring down a strong, healthy stag or roe. And this is where he shows intelligence of the highest order.

When wolves get on the trail of a stag, for example, they follow their prey discreetly—taking care not to alarm him into full flight—until they are near enough to carry out their plan of campaign. One member of the pack after another drops out and takes up his position in hiding in the bushes and undergrowth. One or two strong animals go ahead, moving in a great arc round their victim, so that he is cut off in front. The wretched animal, who naturally has no thought for anything but escape, turns round and goes back the way he came—with a wolf at his heels.

What follows is like a relay race in which one team consists of a dozen wolves, the other of a solitary stag. At the first change-over point the original wolf slackens speed and switches to a steady jogtrot, while the next bounds ahead and continues the chase with new strength. And so it goes on from post to post, until sooner or later one of the wolves manages to get in a nip at the leg which reduces the stag's speed. The stag becomes weaker and weaker until one of the wolves springs at his throat, and hangs on with his immensely powerful jaws. The other wolves close in—and the end soon comes.

But the wolf doesn't always hunt in this manner—only when forced to do so. He takes no pleasure in over-exerting himself, or in making more acquaintance with horns and hooves than he need: he prefers to hunt old, sick or weak animals, which can neither run away nor fight to the death.

On numerous occasions, when I was an executive committee member of the Animal Preservation Association of Alberta, I followed packs of wolves in an aeroplane or helicopter, observing their movements for days on end. Their usual method of hunting is as follows. A pack of twelve to fifteen wolves follows a herd of, for example, wapiti at a distance of about half a mile. If the wapiti stop to graze, the wolves also take a rest. As soon as the wapiti catch the wolves' scent they will take flight; and this is the moment that the wolves have been waiting for. They know very well that in the herd there are almost certain to be animals which for one reason or another are unable to keep up with the rest: because they are old and easily tired, or injured and unable to run fast, or calves that lack the stamina needed to shake off a pack of wolves.

Sooner or later one such animal drops out of the herd and is left farther and farther behind. When the right moment comes the wolves throw themselves on him, and that's that. They eat their dinner, after which they lie down and sleep it off. Next day they resume the pursuit until once again they are about half a mile behind the herd—where they wait expectantly for the next unhappy laggard.

When the wolf starts poaching on human preserves and attacking flocks of sheep or domesticated reindeer, as happens from time to time, there is usually a natural explanation, and one for which we have ourselves to blame. It is only in dire necessity that the wolf will intrude into areas of human habitation, and the commonest cases of dire necessity are when the wolf is starving, or when he is injured and unable to support himself in the usual way. The latter occurs only rarely; for the former we human beings must take the responsibility.

Where the wolf's natural quarry is in adequate supply, he will not trouble us. But when we exterminate the species that form his usual diet he starts attacking domestic animals. And once he has started hunting sheep or domesticated reindeer he is liable to continue, especially if he finds there is little danger involved. After all, it is a simple matter for a wolf to kill a sheep, so why not provide himself with dinner in an easy and effortless way? But where the owners take proper care of their animals, this kind of thing cannot happen.

Although I have never myself seen unmistakable proof, there do seem to have been instances of a wolf getting in among a flock of sheep and carrying out a wholesale and indiscriminate massacre. The key to such cases, I believe, lies in the irritation felt by the intelligent with the stupid. In the wolf's view, while he is busy slaughtering one sheep the rest should be removing themselves as fast and as far as they can. Instead, all they do is to run around in circles like decapitated chickens—so the wolf has to kill another to get them moving. And so it goes on until the poor wolf gives up in sheer desperation.

The best example of the wolf's intelligence and strategic sense that I have encountered occurred that summer I lived among the Ojibwas of northern Ontario. The autumn hunting season had just started, and several of the Indians took jobs as forest guides to hunting parties from the big cities. One of them asked if I would like to go with him on an expedition, and although I am a sworn opponent of hunting for 'sport' I decided to accept his invitation.

As the days went by I got a certain malicious satisfaction from the hunters' lack of success. This lasted until the final day, when they felled a magnificent wapiti. The great beast was skinned, cut up, and dragged to the camp where we were to spend the night. This lay near a great forest lake, on which next morning a seaplane was to land to pick up the hunters.

A large caravan tent had been erected in a little clearing on the edge of the forest. As a rule my Indian friend and I preferred to sleep in the open, but this evening there was a storm brewing, so we decided to move into the tent with the hunting party. The fresh deer meat had been stacked under a spruce and covered, first with the hide, and finally with a huge tarpaulin that we fastened to the ground with tent-pegs.

I had long had the instinctive feeling that wolves were around, but no supporting evidence. Once the daylight had gone, however, the evidence was soon forthcoming. First we heard, quite near, a long-drawn-out call—and then the replies started coming in from every quarter, some from close at hand, others from farther afield. My Indian friend looked at me—this signal and its chorus of answers we knew only too well. It looked like being quite an eventful night.

The Indian suggested that somebody ought to sit outside the tent with a rifle to guard the meat, and the suggestion was taken up. But then the storm broke, a real cloudburst which made it impossible to remain outside and reduced visibility to nil. So the watchman moved into the tent, where he sat with his rifle in his lap trying to keep an eye on the meat—a task rendered quite impossible by the darkness and rain.

Suddenly a fearful concerted howling started up just outside the tent—at least fifteen to twenty wolves in hideous chorus. They were not, however, on the side where the meat was stored, but round the back; and presently they came so close that one of them began scratching at the canvas with his claws. The hunters were visibly nervous—no doubt the old stories about packs of wolves attacking defenceless travellers were flitting through their memories.

There was a window-flap in the back wall of the tent. One of the party posted himself there with his rifle, while another used the only torch we had to try to light up the undergrowth at the back. It was impossible to see anything, but the howling continued without a break. A couple of shots were fired at random without result. Again and again the wolves would make a sortie against the back of the tent, disappearing into the undergrowth as soon as the torch was switched on.

I am not quite sure how long this lasted, but it must have been about two hours. Then the chorus of howling ended as suddenly as it had begun, and it became clear that for some mysterious reason the wolves had left. The whole thing seemed incomprehensible—until one of the hunters ventured out to inspect the meat-store. All he found was the tarpaulin covering—and everything became as clear as day.

The wolves had used what is known in military parlance as diversionary tactics. While the main body had distracted the hunters' attention with their uninterrupted attack on the back of the tent, some of the others had sneaked round to the other side and removed the meat, bit by bit, far into the forest. When the transportation job was completed they had given the signal to their friends, and the attack on the tent had been called off, so that the pack could gather for a well-earned meal in the forest.

The wolf family sticks together in good times and in bad. The mother will give up her life for her young, and the father will fight to the last drop of blood for them all. But courage and intelligence have not been sufficient against man, who has succeeded in wiping out the wolf from large parts of the earth's surface. In the whole of Europe there are now only a few insignificant packs. In the great plains and desolate forests of northern Canada they still survive in large numbers—but for how much longer?

Man in his infinite wisdom has decided that there is no place in nature for the wolf, which constitutes a danger to other forms of animal life. As we saw in the last chapter, the thriving wolf population of the Banff National Park has been exterminated, and now the park-keepers have to slaughter annually several hundred elk, which would otherwise starve to death because the pasture is insufficient to support them.

The world will be a much poorer place without these intelligent and beautiful animals, which play an enormously important part in preserving the balance of nature. One can only hope that man will come to his senses before it is too late—before the last remnants of nature have been obliterated for all time.

One of the most hated animals in North America is the giant cat, known variously as the cougar, puma or mountain lion and equally unpopular under every name. I have tried to understand man's detestation of this cat, but have found no satisfactory explanation, and I have been forced to the conclusion that this is an instance of a characteristic human trait: envy and hatred of any creature that induces feelings of inferiority.

Few hunters succeed in bringing down a cougar without the help of dogs, and very few ordinary people have ever seen one except in a zoo. Even among people who have spent their whole lives in cougar country, perhaps only one in a hundred is lucky enough to have caught even a fleeting glimpse of this proud and beautiful animal—the largest member of the cat family in the North American continent.

I count myself exceptionally fortunate in having seen a great deal of the cougar over the years. Our little ranch in the Clearwater area of Alberta bordered on typical cougar country, and visits from them were frequent. Luckily we had none of the livestock or domestic animals that might have tempted them, and they never bothered us. Human beings they will attack only as a last resource, when it is a question of survival.

In size and colouring the cougar resembles an African lioness (which is a little lighter than an African lion). The back may have a faint brownish tinge, while the belly is a creamy yellow, almost white. The only difference between a cougar and an African lioness is in the shape of the head: the lioness has a broad, blunt snout, whereas the cougar has a beautifully rounded head, like that of a panther or jaguar. The great curved claws are as sharp as razors and the powerful jaws are equipped with a set of terrifying fangs. The strength in these jaws is almost unbelievable—I have seen a cougar crush the head of a dog with a single snap.

46

Like every member of the cat family, the cougar is extremely lithe and graceful in his movements, in spite of the tremendous bunches of muscle distributed around his long slender body. The tail is long and thick, while the legs are powerful and perhaps a little short in relation to the body. The cougar is blessed with that immense strength and suppleness which is unique to the cat family, and I have seen one jump up a ten-foot rock face as easily as our cat jumps on to the living-room sofa.

A cougar is easy to tame if you catch him young enough, before his predator's instincts have taken hold. At this stage he is as cuddly as a kitten; but as he grows up he can become distinctly dangerous to play with. This is not because he is temperamental or hot-tempered, but because he is unaware of his own strength and man's weakness. When, for example, he stretches out a paw to stop a man who is running away, the long, gimlet-sharp claws can shoot out and sink an inch or more into the man's body without the animal being fully aware of it. If the man then continues moving forwards, the result is easy to imagine.

The biggest cougar I ever saw measured nine feet four inches from nose to tip of tail. He weighed nearly sixteen stone. I have heard of even bigger specimens, but the average is around eleven stone, with a length ranging from six feet six inches to eight foot three. A cougar can catch and kill anything (with the possible exception of the grizzly bear), but tends to keep away from other predators. A cougar weighing eleven stone can easily kill a horse seven times that weight—from which it should be clear that a poor little roe deer hasn't the ghost of a chance. And the roe deer is the cougar's main quarry.

Unlike certain other beasts of prey, the cougar never kills more than he can eat. Once he has killed a roe deer or stag, he remains with his booty until he has eaten the last remnants. Where there is plenty of natural prey, some other animals easily become pampered: they kill more than they need, eat the choice morsels, and leave the rest lying around.

A cougar will never attack a man, armed or unarmed, unless he has been wounded by a hunter, or driven into a corner from which there is no escape. He seems to have an

48

instinctive fear of dogs, and when a hunter sets dogs on his trail he takes to his heels without stopping to think. This is something that I have never been able to understand, but I am strongly inclined to believe that it is the dogs' barking and yelping that he is anxious to escape.

If the chase continues long enough, and if there are no rugged mountains near, the cougar usually ends by taking refuge up a tree, where he lies in hope that the dogs will tire and go home. Why he does this is another mystery. He is no doubt aware that the dogs cannot follow him, but he fails to realize that the hunter could pick him off from a safe distance down on the ground. A raccoon would never fall into such a trap.

That the cougar does so is doubly surprising, since in general he is extremely intelligent and a brilliant strategist, as I know from experience. My good friend and neighbour in the Clearwater area, Jack Browning, was a professional big-game hunter. His main occupation consisted of taking parties of hunters out into the wild and guiding them to their prey. What Jack didn't know about nature and wild life wasn't worth knowing. There was only one point on which we disagreed—the merits of the cougar, which Jack hated as much as I admired—and I am convinced that the reason why Jack hated this animal so much was that he felt completely helpless in relation to it.

Jack hunted cougars with specially trained dogs, and over the years he had killed quite a number; but an even larger number had outmanoeuvred him and got away. There was one large old male that he particularly detested. This animal was always around our houses, and I could recognize his tracks out of hundreds of others: he had injured one of his front paws, and the impression made by this paw was quite distinctive. Jack maintained that this cougar was after one of his calves, and indeed he had found the animal outside their enclosure one day. Fortunately for the cougar, Jack was unarmed, so he was able to make his getaway. But Jack determined to hunt him down, and invited me to go with him. I agreed to do so, since I was curious to see his famous dogs in action.

There was a particular bitch that Jack claimed was the

best cougar dog in the whole area. She had had three puppies that Jack had trained with the mother, and these three looked like becoming at least as good as she. Jack decided to give them their baptism of fire; for although the tracks were fresh and therefore easy to follow, the old cougar made up for it by being exceptionally shrewd and experienced.

Together with the bitch and the three puppies we set off into the mountains. Without dogs we would soon have lost the trail, because at the first opportunity the cougar had chosen terrain which showed no footprints. True to form, he had covered a considerable distance at a high speed before easing off and jogging along without too much effort. If you are going to get a cougar between your sights, you have to be prepared to pursue him for hours—often for days.

To begin with, Jack and I kept the dogs on the leash, so that we wouldn't fall too far behind, but as the day went on, and the sun began to sink, the dogs started giving signs that the cougar was now quite near. Either Jack would have to get within range during the next half-hour, or we would have to give up for the day and try to pick up the trail in the morning. The dogs were now almost unmanageable, and Jack decided to take a chance on their being able to keep the cougar at bay until he arrived on the scene. So the four dogs bounded away up the side of the mountain, while we trotted along behind.

Presently we heard a tremendous baying—an indication that the dogs had made contact with the cougar—and we lengthened our stride. The piercing noise came nearer and nearer—then a couple of pitiful howls, followed by silence. I looked at Jack and realized that something was wrong. As a rule, if the dogs stop barking it means only one thing: they have lost the scent completely. But this explanation seemed inconceivable, for the quality of the barking had indicated that the dogs had the cougar in sight, and it would have been impossible for them to lose the trail so quickly. Besides, the whimpering sounds we had heard were incompatible with such a theory.

A moment later we came on a gruesome scene. On a

narrow ledge lay the mutilated bodies of the four dogs. Of the cougar there was no trace, but it wasn't difficult to reconstruct what had happened.

The ledge on which the dogs lay formed a natural passage, with a deep ravine on one side and a hummock of rock on the other. The cougar had traversed the ledge, passing under the hummock of rock. Then he had turned and made a colossal jump on to the hummock, about ten feet above the ledge. There he had lain until the dogs passed beneath him, and stopped. While they stood there uncertain what to do next, the cougar had hurled himself on them from above. The bitch had been killed by a single bite at her head, one of the puppies had had his throat cut, and the spines of the other two had been broken by blows from the cougar's immensely powerful front paws; after which they had been torn to pieces by his claws and teeth.

A badly shaken Jack swore bloody vengeance. And during the next two years he tried again and again to hunt his enemy down. But when I left the area he still hadn't succeeded.

One characteristic which the cougar has in common with the African lion is his refusal to admit another male in the area he regards as his. He marks out this area clearly—which may extend to several square miles—by making scratch marks on trees and moss-grown rocks, digging deep trenches in the ground and throwing up large mounds of earth with his hind legs. On these mounds he urinates, so that there shall be no doubt about whom the land belongs to. If he finds another male cougar within his territory, a battle royal is inevitable.

Another animal that most people regard with loathing and revulsion—again, in my view, unjustly—is the North American coyote. In one respect I can well understand these feelings; but my sympathies are with the coyote. He is, undoubtedly, an incorrigible poultry-thief, and if he gets inside a hen-run you may expect a bloodbath. But it isn't difficult to keep him out, and after several centuries of poultry-farming this fact is just beginning to dawn on the farmers.

The coyote is a distant relation of the wolf, and like the wolf belongs to the dog family. In outward appearance he most closely resembles a fox, though he is somewhat larger. His colouring changes with the seasons: grey and white in winter, yellowy brown in summer, so that he blends naturally with the landscape.

It has been my good fortune to become well acquainted with this extraordinarily intelligent animal, and at one time we had a couple of coyote whelps growing up on our ranch. We never tried to turn them into domestic animals, though this would have been perfectly easy. We let them come and go freely, so that they could get used to their normal environment, and not fall victim to their lack of experience. If we had made pets of them, sooner or later they would inevitably have been killed by the many dogs that ran about the neighbourhood half-wild.

Out in his natural habitat the coyote has little to fear from dogs, and is far too cunning and resourceful for them. His natural prey consists of antelopes and hares, or small rodents, such as voles, that are found in large numbers on the prairie. But he sometimes acquires a taste for sheep and poultry, and for this reason most of the big American sheep farms keep dogs to guard against coyotes. And it is the pursuit of sheep that brings out the coyote's ingenuity most fully.

Although coyotes often hunt on their own, they prefer to work in twos, or in groups of three or four. It is a common practice for one of them to attract the dogs' attention and then take flight with the entire pack at his heels, while his accomplices steal a lamb, which they subsequently divide between them at some remote rendezvous.

The decoy then has to find a means of shaking off his pursuers. He is seldom in any real danger, since he can outstrip all dogs—except the greyhound, which for this reason is used more and more to protect flocks on the prairie. The drawback is that the greyhound has a very poor sense of smell, which means that he is unable to follow a scent, and has to keep his prey in sight.

If the coyote has a greyhound after him, he will make straight for one of the innumerable rainpools that are dotted about the prairie landscape, and roll in the thick layer of algae round the edge of the pool until his coat is completely covered in green scum. Then he creeps quietly and cautiously away through the prairie grass, while the greyhound is left standing helplessly where he last saw his enemy.

To shake off tracker dogs with a keen sense of smell, the coyote resorts to other means. A not uncommon ruse is to find a reasonably fresh cow-pat and plant all four paws firmly in it. The smell of cow-dung more than cancels out the smell of coyote, and the dogs are thrown off the scent.

The coyote is certainly a bloodthirsty little devil and, given the opportunity, he can wreak havoc on sheep and poultry alike. It is, after all, only natural—for animals as well as human beings—to take what is going, in preference to what demands effort and exertion. In his natural element the coyote has a hard life, and he is often hungry. Is it surprising, when a hen-run is left unguarded, that he should go in and help himself? I have heard of one case where a single coyote broke into a poultry farm and slaughtered a hundred and twenty-five birds—out of which he took precisely one when he went on his way. This happened in a place where the hen-run was enclosed by strong fencing. What the farmer had overlooked was the coyote's ability to burrow—the animal had simply tunnelled his way underneath. An electric wire outside the fence would have kept the coyote out effectively.

An acquaintance of mine had a tame coyote which had behaved in an exemplary manner when young, but later acquired a taste for chicken. Since the man kept poultry, he was forced to keep the coyote chained up while the hens were in the yard. In spite of this precaution a hen would disappear from time to time, and the man began to wonder whether he had suspected the coyote unjustly. Then one fine day he discovered the truth.

The coyote was fastened to a chain at the side of the house. He could reach a foot or so round the corner in the direction of the yard, and no farther. The hens kept at a respectful distance from this corner, where they often saw the coyote stretched out, jaws drooling. His dinner used to be brought to him on a tin plate, and one day his scheming mind had devised a master plan.

Cautiously he pushed the tin plate with the remains of his dinner on it just round the corner of the house. Then he drew out of sight and lay concealed. It wasn't long before one or two of the hens yielded to temptation and ventured over to the seductive plate. As soon as the coyote heard their beaks on the bottom of the plate, he sprang round the corner, seized a hen and with a single snap of his jaws launched her into eternity. Then he retreated round the corner again and lay down to enjoy his dinner at leisure.

Coyotes have their regular meeting-places on the prairie, preferably on a hilltop from which they can survey the entire neighbourhood. There they gather in the evening, or on special occasions. But their sociability seldom extends to man, of whom they are instinctively and deservedly afraid.

Nevertheless I have more than once had coyotes running behind my car on a lonely stretch of road in the great forest reserves. On one occasion, when we were snowed up in a blinding storm on a high mountain pass in Montana, my wife had a remarkable experience. I had left her sitting in the car, while I tried to make my way on foot through the storm to the nearest road-maintenance station, a few miles down the road. It was long past dark, and visibility was very poor.

While I was away, she suddenly heard a scratching noise at the car door beside her, turned to the window, and looked straight into the face of what at first she took to be an Alsatian. She rolled down the window, chatted to the animal for a moment or two, and then offered him a biscuit which he ate with a good appetite. She gave him two more, patting his head the while and scratching him behind the ear. By now she realized that he was no Alsatian, though there was something familiar about his appearance. Suddenly it dawned on her: she was petting a real live coyote.

She quickly rolled up the window again, whereupon the coyote loped round to the other side of the car, stood up, and peered in at her from there. Then he vanished back into the storm.

When I returned and she told me what had happened, I

thought at first she was pulling my leg. But on the sheltered side of the car the tracks had not yet been obliterated by fresh snow, and they were, beyond question, the tracks of a coyote. Looking back on the incident, I find no great cause for surprise. This coyote, like other animals I have met with in the wild, may have had some dealings with humans in his younger days, and struck lucky. Some lumberjacks, for example, have taken cubs into their huts for the sake of company, and then turned them loose again before moving on.

If only more people would try to come to terms with nature and make friends with wild animals, the world might become a better place to live in. And I can vouch for the fact that nothing warms the heart more than a wild animal's trust.

A crash from the veranda at the front of the house brought my work to a sudden halt and I gave a routine glance at the clock. The sound was like an earthquake; but an earthquake is felt before it is heard, so I realized at once that this particular earthquake was the work of our friend the Phantom. Evidently he had come for his supper, even if he was almost an hour earlier than usual. To prevent excessive traffic on the veranda I had rigged up a little gate in front of the steps, and to judge by the noise it was this gate that had been pulled down. Indeed, it was not the first time this had happened, and since I had never got round to making it secure I had grown used to a certain amount of commotion every time it was torn down. I decided to scrap it altogether.

The Phantom was a raccoon who had settled on the property and gradually assumed control of our daily routine. He expected to find his supper all ready and served, and he hated to be kept waiting. The only problem was that he was quite unpredictable, since his timetable depended on his stomach. When he was hungry—that is to say, a good deal of the time—he wanted to eat. Still, there were certain more or less regular times of day when he made his appearance on the veranda.

Today, at all events, he was early, a fact which was probably connected with his previous meal. If he had eaten really well in the afternoon, he might lie down and sleep till sunset; but if his meal had been inadequate he would wake early, after which it would not be long before hunger began gnawing at him again.

We lived in a large mountain cabin high up in the San Bernardino range of the Sierra Nevada, about a hundred miles south-east of Los Angeles. It was a two-storey house built on the slope, and under the lower floor a fair-sized ventilation-room had been scooped out of the ground, as is common in southern California. There was more than enough room down there for guests who were not in a position to pay rent. The Phantom lodged in the basement flat, while we lived in the house.

The man we had rented the house from had not been a nature-lover. He couldn't endure animal life anywhere near him, and used to put out poisoned food, so that until we came the wild creatures of the forest had remained at a respectful distance. However, it was not long before the place was full of life and movement again. Animals have a peculiar flair for judging character. They can sense whether a human being is hostile or friendly, and once you have overcome their natural suspiciousness you can win their friendship.

Soon we were receiving regular daily visits from two families of grey squirrels. We also had a couple of chipmunk families, and a multitude of birds, notably blue jays, with their incredibly beautiful colouring and their persistent attempts to steal food from the squirrels.

And then we had the Phantom. He had so many amusing tricks that he could always put me in a good humour, even if at times his exuberance came close to vandalism. The little gate I had rigged up, for example: he could perfectly well have climbed over it—but that never occurred to him. He had to tear it down, even if this was a much more arduous task. In his view the gate was not merely unnecessary but an abomination—a direct contravention of the first law of hospitality. Once he had convinced me of this, and the gate was removed for good, there was the most excellent understanding between us.

In many languages the raccoon is known as the 'washing rat' or 'washing bear'—French *raton laveur*, German *Waschbär*, Norwegian *Vaskebjørn*—because of his supposed habit of washing food before eating it. The truth is that the raccoon lacks the normal salivary glands and is thus incapable of swallowing food such as dry bread or biscuit. Instead, he dips it in water before he puts it in his mouth. True, he sometimes 'washes' other food also, but in general only when it is soiled with sand or pine needles. However, I did once see a raccoon washing a fish he had just caught

in the stream, and since the fish looked juicy enough, this can only have been pure habit.

The raccoon is a rascally little animal about the size of a cocker spaniel, and in many ways he resembles his larger relative, the bear. His hind legs look like bears' paws, and his body is short and round. But unlike the bear he has a long bushy tail, and his head is like a fox's, with a broad forehead and a little pointed snout. It's as if nature wanted to brand him for the robber he is, for his grey face has been provided with a veritable black carnival mask—a broad black band running over the nose, round the eyes, and narrowing towards the ears.

His forelegs are relatively slender and his paws—which are equipped with powerful claws—are almost like a monkey's. It is incredible how much a raccoon can do with these paws. He steals like a magpie—and here his dexterity is a great asset. On one occasion I found the Phantom engaged in unscrewing the lid of a jam-jar he had stolen from the kitchen. I could hardly have done it more quickly or neatly myself.

When he eats, he usually sits on his hind legs and feeds himself with his front paws like a squirrel. He holds the food in one paw, 'washes' it with the other, and then conveys it to his mouth with both paws. It is very seldom that one sees a raccoon eating straight off the ground like other four-legged animals.

From bitter experience he has learned to be wary, for he has many enemies. The worst perhaps is man, who hunts him for his fur. The raccoon has sharp teeth and claws, but since he never weighs more than twenty-two pounds he can't hope to compete with larger animals such as lynxes or wolves—which are also much faster. He therefore compensates for his lack of size, strength and speed by using his brain—and there are many people who consider the raccoon the most intelligent animal to be found in the wild.

Be that as it may, there is no doubt that the raccoon is exceptionally intelligent. Since he is also lazy, he prefers to steal food, when he knows it to be there for the stealing, than go and search for it elsewhere. The Phantom didn't normally steal from us—he didn't normally need to—but it wouldn't surprise me to learn that he stole from others. When all is said and done, thieving is part of a raccoon's nature—which is why he is normally so cordially hated by the farmers on whose land he poaches from time to time.

The raccoon is omnivorous, but his favourite dishes include eggs, fresh chicken and vegetables—especially carrots, tomatoes, turnips and radishes. When he sneaks into a forest farm it is usually the hen-house and the kitchen garden he goes for. Having gorged himself on all the eggs he can lay hands on, he likes to make off with a hen for tomorrow's breakfast, if he is lucky enough to catch one. If he gets into the kitchen garden and isn't chased away pretty promptly it will end a shambles; for he isn't content to pull up a mere two or three carrots. Only the best is good enough, and that means digging up the entire bed in order to select the biggest and juiciest.

On the other hand, if you really want to, you can easily prevent his depredations. You can do what I did—put out the food he needs. For no raccoon would dream of digging or hunting for food unless compelled to do so. Or you can employ a somewhat more brutal method and keep a pair of intelligent dogs on the farm. Although it may be more expensive, my own method is undoubtedly the more certain, since not many dogs can match the raccoon in cunning, fieldcraft or strategy. It is enough to mention two incidents involving friends of mine out in western Canada—in each case farmers who had trained dogs to keep wild animals away.

In one instance a raccoon had managed to get into the farm, unseen, in broad daylight. He was on the point of sneaking into the hen-house when one of the dogs discovered him—and that was the start of a race for dear life. The raccoon set off into the forest with the dogs in hot pursuit. He tried every evasive-action technique known to the raccoon—such as climbing up a tree and out along a branch, and then jumping down on to a convenient knoll. But whatever he did the dogs always found the trail again, because they were so hard on the heels of their prey that they had only to follow their noses.

He would, of course, have been perfectly safe up a tree,

but this is an emergency measure that racoons prefer not to take if possible. The reason is that they associate dogs with man, and they know that if a dog stands under the tree and barks it is only a question of time before the dreaded *homo sapiens* arrives—and against *homo sapiens* they suspect, perhaps, that the tree will offer no protection. In a still more desperate situation they will turn and defend themselves against the dogs as best they can. They doubtless know that they have no real chance against a large dog, but they mean to fight to the death.

On the present occasion the raccoon succeeded in evading the dogs until he was a good distance from the actual farm. Again and again he outmanoeuvred them, but without managing to shake them off—and now the farmer had joined them. However, the raccoon's salvation lay close at hand. He had, perhaps on purpose, followed the same path away from the farm that he had used in approaching it; and now at last came the solution to his problem. He had reached a deep stream, about ten or twelve feet across. Over this stream there was a log, which formed a precarious bridge. Without a moment's hesitation the raccoon ran along the log and was over the stream in a flash; for a raccoon is almost as sure-footed as a squirrel. At first it looked as if he were going to continue helter-skelter into the forest on the other side, but suddenly he turned and calmly surveyed the situation.

The dogs, who had been close behind when he came to the stream, had in the meantime been running up and down along the bank, in search of an alternative place to cross. The stream was too wide to jump, so that the log was the only possibility. One dog opted out at this point, but the other didn't mean to give up so easily. He obviously had no particular desire to try his luck as a tight-rope-walker, but the fever of the chase was upon him—and there at the other end of the log his prey sat waiting. Gingerly he edged his way out along the round log, and all went well until he was halfway across and stood poised for a tremendous leap to safety. But at this decisive moment the raccoon took hold of the end of the log with his two front paws and started rocking it from side to side.

The farmer, who had long since reached the stream, could have settled the matter with a single well-aimed shot; but luckily he was a decent fellow with a sense of humour. And the spectacle he witnessed now was as comical as one could imagine. The dog's desperate attempts to keep his balance were so funny that all the farmer could do was sit down and laugh. He maintains, moreover, that even the raccoon had an unmistakable smile on his little bandit's face. The whole thing lasted only a few seconds: after a series of somersaults the dog landed with a splash in the deep, swift stream. The banks were almost perpendicular at this point, and he had to swim some distance downstream in the icy water before he could reach dry land again—and by then his enthusiasm for the chase had deserted him completely.

I didn't see this incident with my own eyes, but the farmer was a good friend and neighbour, and not the kind of man to make up a story like that, so I see no reason to doubt that it actually happened. I did in any case witness another incident in the same region, and the cunning displayed by the raccoon on this occasion was just as great.

One day early in winter I was down by a forest tarn near our house. Ice had formed, but it was still very thin and brittle. As I stood by the edge, I heard barking noises which came rapidly nearer, until all at once I saw a raccoon come hurtling out of the forest and down to the tarn with a huge watchdog at his heels. They both ran right out on to the ice, which creaked and groaned in protest under their combined weight. Things seemed certain to end badly, because out in the middle the ice looked far too thin to support either the dog or the raccoon. But evidently the raccoon was perfectly aware of this, and indeed the thin ice was an essential feature in his plan of escape.

When he reached the critical point in the middle of the tarn, the racoon lay down flat on the ice and rolled sideways over the delicate part. The ice cracked, but because the raccoon's weight was evenly distributed over a comparatively large surface it held him. It is doubtful if the dog ever stopped to think, such was his eagerness to finish the chase. When he saw his prey lie down and roll on the ice, he gave a couple of tremendous leaps, intending to hurl himself on the fugitive. He landed on all fours in the thinnest part. The ice broke into a thousand pieces, and the dog got a ducking in the ice-cold water which he wouldn't forget in a hurry. While he was struggling to get out, the raccoon strolled off in a calm and dignified manner into the forest on the other side of the tarn.

The raccoon prefers deciduous woods, where there are often hollow tree-trunks in which he can build his home. He has no interest, however, in digging or building a home for himself if he can possibly avoid it, and he prefers to take over a deserted badger's lair or something similar. When forced, he can dig very well; but, as I said before, he is lazy, and his ideal existence consists entirely in eating and sleeping. He does most of his hunting at night, though he may venture out by day if he is hungry enough. He is also often to be seen sunning himself high up in the branches of a tree —where he likes to take over a crow's nest for the purpose.

The Phantom had made himself a really snug, cosy home under our house. At first he was the only animal who came up on to the veranda in search of things to eat, and when we became aware of him we began putting out food at fixed times of the day—mainly in the evening. He never said no to anything, but of course he had his favourite dishes of roast chicken and vegetables. We also gave him plenty of bread and cakes, and we always made sure that his container was filled with fresh water, so that he could moisten the dry food as he ate.

We noticed that he seemed to prefer sweet cakes to other varieties, and this led my wife to try him with a piece of chocolate at supper one day. The result was that he came to demand chocolate as part of his daily menu, and was highly indignant one day when we forgot it. After that I took care always to have a good supply in the kitchen cupboard.

At first, he wouldn't eat if we were out on the veranda, even though he was aware that we watched him through the window. But it wasn't long before he felt completely at ease with us and almost took it for granted that we should sit out and keep him company while he ate. Eventually he would even come up to us and take the morsels that we offered him. He would sit up on his hind legs, hold out his front paws and take the food out of our hands. Then he would put it in his mouth while he shuffled across to his bowl of water, where he washed it thoroughly before eating it. You might have thought it an insult—as if he were casting doubt on our cleanliness.

One day we noticed that he had acquired a new habit. Having eaten part of his food, he would carry the rest down below, making several journeys, and always reserving the choicest morsels for this purpose. There has never been any evidence that raccoons hoard food; and in any case what he took away was not the sort of thing that would keep for long in the warm climate of the Sierra Nevada. We began to wonder whether the Phantom had got into the way of laying the breakfast table down in his living quarters before setting out on his nocturnal wanderings.

However, the mystery was cleared up one day when he arrived for lunch accompanied by another raccoon—clearly a female. She had been living down there all the time, and the reason why she hadn't ventured upstairs for her meals was, as subsequent developments showed, that while the Phantom was consolidating his friendship with us, she had been lying in childbed. Besides, he had wanted to make quite sure there were no hidden dangers before bringing her out into the light of day. In this hard world you can never be too careful.

It was not long before she became even more at ease with us than the Phantom had been; and if my wife was late with supper she would shuffle trustfully into the kitchen to lend a helping paw. But both of them continued taking food to their home downstairs—which made it clear beyond doubt that our family had grown, and that the basement now housed a Phantom junior.

Finally—many weeks after we had first made the Phantom's acquaintance—the great day came when we were allowed to see our friends' offspring. This turned out to be an experience such as few people are granted more than once in a lifetime. We had more or less expected to catch a glimpse of the youngster playing with his mother and father outside the house; instead, his proud parents decided to bring him with them up to the veranda and introduce him properly.

Early one evening we heard a tremendous hullabaloo on the veranda. We opened the door and found the Phantom waiting for us. It was obvious that he had some very definite purpose in mind, so we went out and sat on the veranda bench; whereupon the Phantom ran to the top of the steps, got up on his hind legs and started beckoning with one of his front paws. A moment later we heard a rustling and a rumbling, and up popped the mother. At her side was her young son, his little head just visible as he stretched up to see what lay before him. He had some difficulty negotiating the high veranda steps, and needed a little help from his mother; but eventually all three of them stood before us. I have seldom seen anything to equal the pride that shone from the parents' eyes; and their son was indeed one of the most enchanting little creatures that it is possible to imagine. His legs were still a little thin and wobbly, but in every other respect he was a perfect miniature edition of his proud father. After this solemn ceremony of presentation something special seemed to be called for—and we celebrated the occasion with chocolate all round. Presently we were even allowed to pat the little fellow.

He showed virtually no fear of us, but he was never allowed to visit us on his own—either his father or mother insisted on coming too. Nor, when we were all together on the veranda, was he allowed to come up to us by himself— one or other of his parents had always to accompany him. As time went on he sometimes seized the chance of breaking bounds and sneaking up the veranda steps while his parents were otherwise engaged; but if he was caught in the act he earned a good cuffing. It was not that the Phantom and his wife imagined we would harm the youngster, but each of them had doubtless had some bitter experiences with the human race in general. It was therefore essential that from childhood onwards he should learn to be cautious in his dealings with man—or childhood might be the only state he would enjoy. Even if he occasionally played truant and visited us on the quiet, he evidently understood the lesson his parents were trying to teach him because, when we had visitors, neither he nor they ever showed up—even though I knew perfectly well where they could be found.

The autumn we shut up house and left Big Bear Lake was in many ways a sad one; in particular, we often think of our raccoon family, and wonder what has become of them.

It was my wife who was responsible for bringing a skunk into the family. Having had some slight acquaintance with skunks in their natural state, I must admit to having begun by expressing doubts; but even my mild protests were silenced when I set eyes on the little heart-breaker, to whom Ciska gave the appropriate name of Sniffy. Over the years he gave us so much happiness and pleasure that we never regretted taking him in.

A well-known American scientist once declared that whoever chose the eagle as the symbol of the United States showed very poor judgment: he should have chosen the skunk. The eagle, he pointed out, is not typical of American animal life, and in addition it is found in the emblems of several other nations. Furthermore, the eagle is a bird of prey. He gives a false impression of the American disposition, conveying as he does the feeling that at any moment he is about to hurl himself at some unsuspecting, defenceless victim.

The skunk, on the other hand, is a typical North American animal, found all over the continent. He is handsome, intelligent, high-principled, fearless, good-natured and friendly. He never attacks without provocation; but if forced to defend himself he can do so with a weapon so fearful that even the largest and most powerful enemies maintain a respectful distance. Every animal in the forest seems to know about this weapon, and consequently leaves him in peace.

After my first unfortunate encounter with a skunk, it was a long time before I could accept this glorification of an animal capable of producing so indescribable a smell. But later, when I got to know skunks really well—both wild and tame—I came round completely to the scientist's view.

There are several species of skunk, but the most common is the striped variety, known as the Canadian skunk, who is found in almost every part of North America, from the Mexican border up to the north Canadian tundra. He is the same size as an average cat but has a very distinctive build. His head, which is shaped like an acute-angled triangle, with a broad forehead and a narrow snout, is disproportionately small in relation to his body. His ears are round and rather small, and his body is almost pear-shaped, with the narrowest part in front. His hips are like those of the Venus de Milo, his hind legs short and powerful, and his front legs even shorter and equipped with substantial claws for digging. His thick, long-haired coat is as smooth as silk, with a brilliant gloss. On either side of his back are two broad white stripes which begin together at the forehead, divide at the neck, and meet again at the root of the tail. The rest of his coat is coal-black. His tail is as long as his body, and is a beautiful sight when spread out above the back like a fan. It is white on top and black on the under-side.

The two scent glands are placed just beneath the tail, one on each side. It is often said that to squirt his evil-smelling fluid the skunk has to have both hind legs firmly on the ground, and that to prevent him from using his weapon all you have to do is lift him by the tail. I have never put this theory to the test, nor would I encourage others to do so. It might well be wrong—or the skunk might refuse to let you grasp his tail. As he is extremely quick on the turn, you would have to ask his permission first.

As I mentioned above, the animals of the forest seem to have an instinctive awareness of the skunk's homely weapon. This awareness, however, is apparently denied to dogs, especially town dogs—which is why it is mainly dogs that make the involuntary acquaintance of the skunk's brand of perfume. Our own elkhound, Bamse, was one of these unfortunates; and on that occasion he learned a lesson that lasted him all his life.

It happened when we were out on one of our daily walks in the forest near our home in western Canada. Suddenly Bamse disappeared into the undergrowth to investigate something. There he found a wild skunk which he no doubt mistook for his good friend and playmate, Sniffy. When the skunk showed no reaction to his usual introductory atten-

tions, Bamse doubtless began to suspect that something was wrong; and to get to the bottom of the matter he did what dogs commonly do and thrust his nose under the skunk's tail. The touch of the dog's cold damp nose in a private place was a bit too much for the peaceful skunk, which till then had been remarkably patient, and he fired with both barrels. Then he wandered away, calmly and with dignity, in search of some undergrowth where he wouldn't be disturbed.

Meanwhile Bamse's dignity had entirely deserted him. He howled with pain as he rolled on the ground, rubbing his face in the grass to get the abominable stuff out of his nose and eyes. The shock, and the total blindness induced by the fluid, made him almost out of control, but eventually I got the lead on him and began the long trek home. Very little of the fluid had actually gone in his eyes, but even so it was almost an hour before his sight returned. As for myself, how I got home I hardly know, because the smell from Bamse was so nauseating that I almost passed out every time I drew breath.

It took a whole week of daily sessions with turpentine before we got the smell out of his coat. But the worst of all, from Bamse's point of view, was that during that period Sniffy refused to have any dealings with him—he too found the stench intolerable.

The one-act play the two of them performed on our return home was so comic that we almost forgot the unpleasant aspects. There was no question of bringing Bamse into the house. Instead, I took him through the gate into the garden—and there was Sniffy. As soon as Bamse caught sight of him with his swollen, smarting eyes, he ran up, tail wagging, intending to give him his usual lick of salutation. He was still a yard or two away when Sniffy smelled him, backed away in disgust, and finally turned tail and fled as fast as his legs would carry him. Bamse stood as if paralysed, while his face reflected the most heart-rending sorrow at being abandoned in the hour of need by his best friend. It was a crestfallen and apathetic dog who slunk after me to the far end of the garden for the first instalment of the cleansing process.

The skunk has an amazing accuracy of aim, and can hit his target at ranges of up to five and six yards. Beyond that distance the spray is too diffused to have quite the same devastating effect. The maximum range is about eight or nine yards, though with a favourable wind the intense smell will carry up to half a mile or so. After the first dose the skunk can manage another three or four gradually diminishing bursts, until finally he runs out of ammunition. After that it takes him several hours to recharge.

It is evident that the skunk prefers not to have to use his weapon except in the direst necessity. If attacked by another animal, a dog for example, he first tries to scare away the aggressor. With lowered head and a grim expression, he charges forward in the dog's direction. Then he stops short, shoots his tail up and forward over his body like a spread fan, stamps violently with both front legs three times in rapid succession, and retires to his starting-point. If the dog continues to make sorties against him, he will repeat this curious counter-attack once or even twice, and remain in the on-guard position.

If the aggressor now has the wit to take himself off, the incident is closed. But if he resumes the offensive, the next round is short and swift. The skunk plants his front legs firmly on the ground, shoots up his tail, and does a somersault on his front legs, directing his hind-quarters at the attacker. As the back legs hit the ground he fires—and the battle is over. If the attacker is blinded it can last for anything from half an hour to three or four hours, depending on the size of the dose; and the accompanying pain is very intense.

The skunk is a nocturnal animal, sleeping or resting most of the day and hunting by night. He lives mainly on the smaller rodents of the woods and fields, supplementing this diet with root crops and insects. He digs his hole under tree roots, boulders and old buildings, and in the colder parts of North America he hibernates all winter. He is a first-rate mouser, and he often settles on a farm, making his lair under one of the outbuildings, and keeping the stables and cowsheds free from mice and rats. The farmer seldom has any objection to this arrangement, and it is not uncommon for a skunk to be virtually adopted as a farm animal, ambling freely in and out of the kitchen for his daily bowl of milk.

It is usual, when adopting a skunk as a domestic animal, to take the precaution of having him 'deodorized' by the surgical removal of his scent glands; but in that case the owner must remember that the poor skunk is now completely at the mercy of larger animals. The skunk makes an excellent pet, being manageable and even-tempered, and very clean in his habits. He is as faithful as a dog and as cuddly as a cat, besides being playful and full of mischief. He can also adapt himself to a household in which there are other animals.

Sniffy was a good example of this. He was only four weeks old when we acquired him, and we already had two dogs and two cats, all of whom immediately accepted him as an amusing addition to our large family. It was not long before Sniffy dominated the house—the only creature he showed respect for being the elder cat, who in turn regarded Sniffy with condescending friendliness, varied on occasion with supreme contempt.

Shortly after his arrival, our bitch had a litter of eight puppies, and Sniffy was in his element. It was impossible to keep him away from them, although in playing with him they were often very rough. His razor-sharp teeth could easily bite through a man's finger, but with the puppies he was so careful that they never got so much as a scratch, even though Sniffy himself was often scratched till he bled.

We tried to keep Sniffy on the go all day, in the hope that he would get into the habit of sleeping at night like the other inhabitants of the house. As long as there was something to occupy him all was well; otherwise he would keep dozing off, and then he would be full of energy all night long. It was amazing what he could get up to in the course of a night, and after a series of dearly-bought experiences we built a wire cage, where he slept in a bed of straw and rags which he made for himself. He also stole one of my wife's slippers, refused to go to sleep without it, and was finally allowed to keep it. After that he slept with his head in this slipper every single night until he died.

In the fullness of time we provided Sniffy with a mate—

whom we called Chanel. It was then that we made an unexpected discovery: that skunks dance at full moon. Sniffy had never done this until Chanel came into his life, so it seems likely that skunks only do it when they are two or more. One evening when they were playing together, Chanel suddenly got up on her front legs and danced round in circles with her tail-end sticking up in the air. A moment later Sniffy too began dancing—but he performed on his hind legs. This became a regular ritual between them whenever the moon was full; and later I discovered that it was a common practice among wild skunks also. I once saw a group of five families, totalling more than twenty animals, dancing around on their hind legs in the moonlight.

The skunk shows the same kleptomania as a crow or magpie, and he cannot resist bright, shiny objects. Sniffy thought nothing of stealing when the occasion offered. If my wife missed a ring or some other ornament, there was seldom any doubt about where it had got to. We only needed to go down to the cellar and search in Sniffy's cage, and almost invariably we would find the missing object hidden somewhere in his bed.

Sniffy was full of tricks. When the dogs were asleep, he loved to creep up on them from behind, take hold of one of the tufts of hair between their toepads, and give it a good tweak. When the dog started up and looked round for the offender, Sniffy would sit facing the other way, all innocence. This could go on for hours on end—to the intense irritation of the unfortunate dogs.

The skunk is an easy animal to feed: he is perfectly content with scraps from the master's table, and has no objection to dog food. Like every other creature, however, he has his favourite dishes, and these include raw meat and egg yolks. He prefers milk to water, and as far as Sniffy was concerned the milk always tasted better if it had been filched from the cats. If we felt he had earned a bonus, we would give him a handful of peanuts or a couple of dog biscuits.

Sniffy was ready to fight for his rights, and he himself laid down the rules about what these were. If he had taken something that belonged to another—man or beast—he then regarded it as his property, which he was prepared to defend; and if the other disputant was somebody he disliked he could be pugnacious to a degree.

At that time my wife and I were both fully occupied, and we therefore employed a domestic help. She was married, and Sniffy detested her husband—and made his detestation unmistakable from the word go. One Sunday we had asked them both in for coffee, and my wife had made a cream cake —which happened to be one of Sniffy's favourite delicacies. While the husband sat fiddling with the television set, Sniffy sneaked up to the little table by his chair, reached up on his hind legs, and snatched his piece of cake. At that very moment the man turned round, and instinctively put out his hand to rescue it. In a flash Sniffy seized his forefinger and gave a vicious bite. The unfortunate man hopped about sucking his finger—which proved to have been bitten right through—while Sniffy proceeded to eat the cake as though nothing had happened. He would never injure anyone he liked, or who had treated him kindly, and this particular man later admitted that he had deserved what he got. He had always teased and tormented Sniffy whenever he had the opportunity.

A tame skunk is almost as loyal as a dog, and if he has once given his affection to a human being nothing can alter him. He is basically a one-person animal, though sometimes he will admit a second person to his heart. Sniffy and I were the best of friends, but his affection for my wife bordered on adoration. What he liked best in the world was to lie draped over her shoulders, licking her behind the ears with his little red tongue. He knew his name and came instantly when called. When my wife's footsteps were heard outside, Sniffy would run to the door to be the first to welcome her home again.

Unfortunately, although the skunk has excellent hearing and sense of smell, he is exceptionally shortsighted and is easily blinded by bright light, with the result that every year large numbers of skunks are run over at night. But a motorist who has had the misfortune to run over a skunk learns a lesson he is unlikely to forget in a hurry, and may become a more cautious driver in future. It makes no difference how quickly the skunk dies after being hit:

in the very instant of death he fires a volley of his malodorous fluid, and the motorist is lucky if he ever gets the smell out of his car again.

I know of no other animal, with the possible exception of the wolverine, who is more fearless than the skunk. A deodorized skunk, as mentioned before, may be an easy victim to dogs, since he will not back down and does not seem to realize that his weapon is useless. Sniffy might have been in serious trouble many times but for his trusted friend Bamse, who was always there to protect him.

I have always been amazed at the way nature seems to depend on a system of self-help. Man has thought it increasingly necessary to come barging in with his improvements and modernizing, but there are still parts of the world in which he has not yet found it profitable to introduce technology. In these areas nature still has to fend for herself—and to maintain, for example, her own sanitation department.

Such areas are to be found in the tropical zones of Africa and America, and in Andalusia in southern Spain. And the sanitation department I have in mind consists of the carrion-eating birds, especially their king, the vulture.

It was in Andalusia that I had my first real opportunity of studying the vulture at close quarters. The vulture needs three things: high mountains, a scorching sun, and a plentiful supply of unburied carcases. All three are particularly abundant in Andalusia.

The vulture not merely enjoys the heat of the sun, it is absolutely necessary to him. This is because he needs to fly high enough to have an unimpeded view of a vast area. He has first to reach a height of about ten thousand feet, at which he glides in great circles on motionless wings for hours on end. This routine he repeats two or three times a day according to circumstances. Since a full-grown vulture weighs anything from about eighteen to twenty-two pounds, this high-altitude flying involves an enormous output of energy. To accumulate the calories that he would consume in soaring to such a height three times a day by his own unaided efforts, he would need to eat nine times his own weight in meat—and that, of course, is impossible.

This is where the sun is an indispensable ally. Long after eagles, falcons, buzzards, chicken hawks and other birds of prey have gone out in search of food, the vulture sits on his mountain ledge and waits till the sun has warmed the ground sufficiently to set in motion the current of warm air that will carry him up to the great heights he needs. He seems to know exactly when the current is strong enough to support him, and when the moment arrives he hurls himself from his ledge, spreads his mighty wings, and rises steadily with the current until he reaches the required height. Here he hovers while he begins his search for food. The height is determined by the strength of the air current, and the area within which he circles by his distance from neighbouring vultures—for they are collaborators and competitors at one and the same time.

Throughout this book I refer to animals as 'he' in preference to the pedantic 'he or she' (or the insultingly lifeless 'it'). In the case of the hovering vulture, however, 'he' is almost certainly correct. The female is usually in the nest with her chick, which needs constant care and attention. Vultures never have more than one chick at a time, and the mother lays an egg only every second year, because the chick needs at least a year before he can fend for himself. And the father always takes care that the family is not too large to be adequately fed.

As he circles high in the heavens, the vulture looks like a single vast wing. His wing-span is not far short of ten feet, and each wing measures over two feet across. The tail is short and broad, which is no disadvantage, since in any case the vulture has no energy to squander on aerobatics. The head is extremely hard to discern, even with a powerful telescope, because of the vulture's habit of retracting it, as a protection against cold, inside the ruff of feathers round the lower neck. It resembles an eagle's, except that it is completely bare of plumage. The short yellow claws are blunt and virtually useless for tearing or carrying. The colouring is uniformly drab, except for the ruff, which is coffee-coloured, and the primaries, which are black.

The fact that only one vulture is visible circling in the sky does not mean that he is alone. On the contrary, it is safe to assume that there are dozens of them, each surveying his allotted area. Vultures depend on one another, and they watch one another. To conserve their strength they keep strictly, as if by agreement, to their appointed positions. As

long as each one continues circling, his neighbours know that the dinner-table has not been laid in *that* sector. But if one of them dives, the others know instantly that he has found food and hurry to join him.

The vulture has fantastically keen eyesight, which enables him to see everything that goes on down on the ground, from a height of up to ten thousand feet. But there is a riddle that has not yet been finally solved: how does the vulture know that his victim is dead—that the animal lying far below him is not just asleep? He cannot afford to waste his strength by swooping down to investigate. He has to be certain; and he never makes a mistake. It isn't long, of course, before the dead body of an animal starts to smell in the strong, tropical sun; but this isn't the explanation, since—perhaps luckily for him—the vulture has a very poor sense of smell. It seems clear that he relies entirely on his eyesight. But what does he see?

The best explanation of this phenomenon that I have heard came from an old Spanish swineherd, who had lived all his life in typical vulture country, and who reckoned that the decisive factor was the vulture's powers of observation. In the oppressive heat of an Andalusian summer day animals often sleep like the dead. But they normally do so as a flock or a herd, and at fixed times and places, from which they seldom depart. The vulture too has his fixed station, where he remains day in, day out, often for weeks on end. He studies the ground below him until he knows every detail in the landscape. In addition, he studies the habits of the animal population, until he knows them better than the animals do themselves. And if he sees an animal lying alone and apart from the others his interest is immediately aroused.

Again and again in the course of the day he observes with minute attention the animal down there on the ground. His circling becomes narrower and narrower, though his altitude remains constant. At sunset he flies away and probably forgets the whole thing. But next day he is back again in the same place. The animal is still lying there, and the vulture is now more interested than ever. He is also hungrier, and he has no desire to go home once again to his wife and child with nothing for dinner. He flies a little lower, watching for a movement in the body—for some indication that the animal is alive or dead. But he goes on waiting, for he has no intention of making an unnecessary landing. It is widely believed that the vulture prefers rotten meat, but the truth is that he often has no choice. It takes at least two days before he can be sure that the body down there is well and truly dead—and by that time, in a tropical climate, it is very likely that the process of decomposition has already begun.

He circles lower and lower. The other vultures observe his manoeuvres and begin closing in. This gives him an added impetus. But he is still searching for some indication that will put the case beyond doubt. Suddenly he finds what he is looking for—it may be the swollen, protruding tongue, or perhaps the open eyes, with the whites showing —and comes in for the landing.

He lands a few yards away, approaches crabwise, then hops and shuffles round the body, though he doesn't come too near. Throughout all this he keeps his body erect and his wings partly spread, with the tips sweeping the ground. His head moves rapidly from side to side as he scrutinizes the corpse, first with one eye, and then with the other.

If he had had any sense of smell at all, there would by now have been no doubt in his mind that the animal was long since dead. But there is still a residual fear that inhibits him from claiming his rights—until, that is, a large shadow falls over him. He looks up, sees a swarm of his fellows coming in to land, leaps into the air and plunges his beak into the carcase.

Then he jumps hurriedly back to see the result of his action, and when nothing happens he emits a croaking sound and hurls himself forward again. Taking a good grip on the skin of the abdomen, he uses his powerful legs and wings to thrust his entire weight backwards, and so tears off a strip of skin. Then he hacks and tears at the exposed abdomen to get at the vitals—heart, liver and lungs—which he regards as a special delicacy.

Suddenly he finds himself being assisted by dozens of other vultures, all pushing and pulling and fighting to get their heads in the animal's abdominal cavity. Now it becomes clear why the head and neck have to be naked. As the swineherd said: 'It's the one part of the body that he can't clean for himself. If it had been covered in plumage, he'd soon have been full of worms that would have eaten him alive.' The swineherd's description of the vulture was a vivid one: *'an eagle with rolled-up shirtsleeves'*.

From every corner of the heavens there descend fresh swarms of hungry vultures, until the carcase is covered with a solid mass of flapping wings and toiling bodies. The late-comers sit in trees or on the ground, waiting for their turn to join in the feast. At the height of the banquet there are nearly a hundred birds gathered round the carcase, or what is left of it. Once they start they make quick work of it: the old swineherd told me that they finish off a mule in about two hours, an ox in three.

As they near the borderline between satiety and distension, the first arrivals drop out one by one. At first, they can hardly move, let alone fly; all they can do is sit there and let the food subside. They lean back on their broad strong tails, and slowly fan themselves with their wings. Their beaks hang open. From time to time they give a great belch. By the end of an hour the meal has settled in their stomachs.

Now it is time for our friend to be off home to his family. With heavy, clumsy movements he shambles along the ground and flexes his mighty wings. Eventually he takes off, finds himself a suitable air current, and swings himself in ever widening circles up and up into the mountains.

Landing on a ledge close to his eyrie, he regurgitates his entire dinner. Helped by his wife, he uses his beak to sort out all the choicest morsels, which she then puts greedily away. When her hunger is appeased, she opens her mouth as wide as it will go and allows her youngster to help himself freely from her gizzard. Remnants left lying on the ledge go to the father, but any such second helping is nearly always pitiably small.

By now the male bird is hungry again, so off he sets once more to take advantage of the last of the daylight in his everlasting search for food for himself and his family.

Presently he is back at his post, circling round on top of his chosen air current, glassy-eyed as he spies out the land for his next meal.

Few creatures have been more shamefully misjudged than the vulture. His way of life is one that we cannot help finding repulsive. But if we knew more about him, we would surely find many redeeming features.

Very little information about this mighty bird is available, and of that little a large proportion is distorted. When we see a character in a film stumbling through the desert half-dead with thirst, and a flock of vultures swarming round him and pouncing on him as he stumbles, the whole scene is pure fantasy. The vulture has no offensive or defensive weapons of any kind—which is why, unlike his cousin the eagle, he is unable to attack a living creature. Once he is down on the ground, he is completely defenceless. Thus it is from necessity, not from choice, that he waits until his prey is dead.

When the vultures have finished with a carcase, only the bones remain, and these are taken care of by a host of other sanitary workers: worms, ants, termites and beetles, who come swarming out of the ground and set to work on the skeleton. Within a matter of days this too has vanished, and there is nothing left to show that an animal died here less than a week before.

It is thanks to the vulture and the other carrion-eating birds, together with their myriad helpers in the insect world, that we are spared the waves of pestilence and epidemics that occur all too easily when animal carcases are simply left to rot. The vulture deserves, not contempt and revulsion, but a memorial in token of services rendered.

ELEVEN CONDOR, RELIC FROM THE PAST

The legendary 'thunder bird' of the Indians has been flying over southern California for more than a million years. Those who venture into the wild landscape of Los Padres National Park, north of Los Angeles, can still see him hovering high over the mountains.

This giant among birds—the wing-span of the Californian condor is approximately ten feet and he weighs more than twenty-two pounds—is far and away the largest terrestrial bird in North America; the turkey-buzzard (or turkey vulture) and the golden eagle are both small by comparison. It is not his size, however, that makes him unique, but the fact that he is an anachronism. He existed in California before the ice age, living off deceased mastodons. But somehow or other he contrived to outlive his prehistoric contemporaries, and we can still see him today, hovering on powerful wings over the very same mountains in which his ancestors hatched out their eggs a million years ago.

Unfortunately the thunder-bird's future is not very bright. The American Ministry of Agriculture and the National Audubon Society have estimated the total number of condors in North America at no more than forty, all of them living in a special protected area of about eighty square miles known as the Sespe Condor Reserve, within Los Padres National Park. Of the forty surviving birds it is believed that only ten pairs are at present capable of continuing the species, the others being young birds below the age of reproduction. When one considers that the condor only hatches out a single egg every other year, and that four or five birds die annually, it will be seen that the stock has little chance of increasing.

The California condor is a distant relative of the condor that lives in the Andes, the essential difference being that the latter will attack living animals and birds and kill them, whereas the California condor, like every other species of vulture, lives exclusively on carrion. He is incapable of killing and therefore has to search for dead beasts down on the ground. But finding them is not enough: they must be accessible, and this poses a problem. Because of his enormous wing-span and his need for a runway of at least twenty yards when he takes off again after landing, carcases in the forest are of no use to him: they have to lie in the open or on mountain ledges.

Like all members of the vulture family, condors search for food in teams. When they have found a carcase they land a short distance away and amble up to it. If a golden eagle is already on the scene, the condor waits at a respectful distance until the eagle has eaten; for although the condor may be nearly twice the eagle's size he respects the eagle's powerful back and sharp claws. On the other hand, the condor won't give way to the turkey-buzzard, which is quite as big as the eagle. It is the turkey-buzzard who sits a little way off and waits until the condor's appetite is satisfied.

It takes a good year before the condor's chick can fend for himself, although he is full-grown after about seven months, by which time he needs as much food as his parents. So his parents need virtually a year's break in which to recuperate.

Where parental duties are concerned, the condor couple appear to practise sexual equality, with the father taking his full part in bringing up the young. The couple don't build nests, but find themselves a snug, moss-lined cave or cranny high up on the face of the mountain, in which the female lays her egg. The egg is large—about three times the size of an average hen's egg—with a light, grey-green colouring. During the six weeks' incubation period the parents take it in turns to sit; and when the chick is hatched they both go and scavenge for food, the youngster being fed generally once a day.

With the best will in the world one couldn't call the condor a beautiful bird. He lives on death and decay, and his outward appearance, appropriately enough, is a death's head. The beak is long and hooked, the bare skin on the head and

neck is the colour of saffron, and the eyes are lit by a diabolical crimson gleam.

Sitting on the ground or up on his mountain perch, the condor looks awkward, almost grotesque. But as soon as he spreads his mighty wings and soars into the heavens he is transfigured, becoming a creature of almost poetic beauty. A condor in flight is a spectacle one never forgets. He is an aeronautical masterpiece, perfected thousands of years before man's earliest ancestors began to develop human characteristics. With his wing tips he can discern the tiniest change in the currents of air that support him, and he can stay suspended for hours on end without making the slightest movement of his wings.

The condor has seldom been short of food in the areas he has made his own. In addition to the wild life in which these regions are rich, there are large numbers of cattle and sheep who stray from the surrounding ranches into the wilderness, and who sooner or later fall victim to the elements and the dangers of the wild. Why, then, is this majestic bird almost extinct?

The answer is man, and man's urge to kill. This harmless giant has never been a threat to man or his interests—quite the reverse. And with one bizarre exception, man has never been able to make use of a dead condor. Nevertheless, whenever he finds himself near a condor he seems unable to keep his finger off the trigger. The worst slaughter took place in the 1850s, at the height of the California Gold Rush. The prospectors discovered that the shaft of the condor's enormous wing feathers was a convenient receptacle for gold dust. In fact a shaftful of gold dust became a standard measurement in the goldfields—'a quill of gold', as it was called. And in order to supply the prospectors with the wing feathers they needed, hundreds of adult condors were killed.

After the gold-diggers, the worst inroads on the condor population were made by the cattle-breeders. When their animals perished out in the wilds, they erected traps round the carcases. These were intended for the wolves, lynx and coyotes that often ravaged the herds of cattle, but they also caught large numbers of condors, which were either maimed or held captive until they were put out of their misery by wild animals or human beings.

Today the condor is protected all the year round, and there are severe penalties for anyone caught killing one. Nevertheless certain people seem incapable of leaving them in peace. A man was arrested after shooting a condor as recently as 1964; his somewhat lame excuse was that he had mistaken it for a mere turkey-buzzard.

How to preserve for posterity the last little colony of California condors is a much-debated problem. The bird's champions are divided into two camps, one advocating a strict policy of non-intervention, the other that the birds should be helped by providing food near their nests. Until now the non-interventionists have had the upper hand, but the strongest arguments seem to be against them. There may well be a shortage of food in the area where the birds are nesting, since it has now become a protected area and is thus frequented only by ordinary game. In the absence of cattle or sheep the condors may have to fly considerable distances to find something to eat. They have been observed more than a hundred miles from their mountain eyries, in places which they can only have reached by flying over open hunting grounds, where they are in perpetual danger, especially during the hunting season.

It makes very little difference to the condor whether the carcase is, as it were, imported, or home-produced. And if he had enough food in his own territory he wouldn't need to search elsewhere—and so would escape the menace of the trigger-happy hunter.

Another possible way of preserving the condor for posterity is to capture a pair of young birds and get them to breed in captivity. This has been successfully tried with the condor from the Andes; and the zoo at San Diego houses a number of these birds, which have mated and hatched eggs just as they would have done in their natural surroundings. This method must be used, of course, only as a last resource. For myself, I am opposed to any form of captivity for wild animals, but in this instance it may be preferable to the alternative of complete extinction.

TWELVE

Many species of animal have already disappeared from the surface of the earth, and others are on the point of doing so. They are exterminated systematically, for gain, or from pure ignorance. Few people wish to see the extinction of the animal world around them—though concern is likely to centre on those species which have a wide popular appeal. In Britain, for example, there would be a public outcry if the government announced a bounty on red deer or otters; but very few tears would be shed over the news that the last adder in the country had, as it is euphemistically called, been 'put down'. The adder does nothing to attract our sympathy, and so most of us care little whether he is exterminated or not. We overlook the vital fact that every creature on this earth has a purpose, a part to play in maintaining the balance of nature. And this remains true whether or not we like the creature in question.

One of the vanishing species is the American alligator. Some may regard him as an unattractive creature; but, for all that, he performs a very important function. Man has had few dealings with the alligator, and consequently knows very little about him. This is a pity, because the alligator is a most interesting character and well worth a closer acquaintance.

Today, if you want to find an alligator in his natural surroundings, you will have to travel far into the swamps of the southern states of America. The main reason for his near-extermination was the tremendous demand for shoes and handbags made of alligator skin. Alligators were shot by the thousand, with no regard for their ecological function —their indefatigable consumption of the animal carcases which lay rotting in the swampy waters, and which, but for them, would sooner or later have led to outbreaks of plague.

One result of this insanely excessive levy on the alligator population has been that alligator skin is no longer to be found on the market. Today, when a woman proudly displays her 'real alligator' shoes or handbag, you can be sure that the skin comes from the South American caiman—a relative of the alligator that still survives in large numbers, especially in the immense Amazon valley.

My first encounter with an alligator in his natural surroundings took place in the almost impenetrable swamp area known as the Everglades, in the southern part of the Florida peninsula. It is along the banks of the swampy rivers and pools that one is most likely to find them, although they are extremely shy. The alligator likes to lie stock-still on the bank and bask in the sun. He takes no notice of natural everyday sounds; but at the slightest unfamiliar noise he glides swiftly and silently under the water and into his hole, which is always in the bank of the swamp near his chosen sun-bathing place. The entrance is just below water level, but the hole itself is above. Before going into hiding, he lies expectantly for a moment outside his hole, with only his nose and eyes above the surface of the water, trying to identify the sound. Then he glides into the hole, where he lies and waits until his unbelievably keen sense of hearing tells him that the danger is past.

I had found a fine specimen, a good ten feet in length, and had finally come close enough to raise my camera. The tiny click was enough to send him headlong into the water, and I had no choice but to wait for him to reappear. I sat between the bushes, as quiet as a mouse, while swarms of mosquitoes had a banquet at my expense. But my patience was at last rewarded. After an interminable delay my friend came up on the bank again and stretched himself out in his usual place, a mere five yards away. There he lay as if he were dead; for like all cold-blooded reptiles he generates no thermal energy, and therefore avoids moving more than is absolutely necessary.

Suddenly, a large wading bird came flying over the swamp, just above water level, as they mostly do when hunting for frogs or small fishes, and flew past the alligator on the bank at a distance of a foot or two. Faster than the eye could follow, the apparently dead alligator lunged sideways—and the bird was caught between his immensely powerful jaws.

And now I witnessed a truly amazing drama. The alligator's teeth are conical in shape and lack both biting edges and masticating surfaces, so that he is incapable of chewing his prey. Since the throat is very narrow, he is incapable also of swallowing anything much bigger than a man's fist, and when he catches anything as big as a wader he needs help.

My alligator now produced a grunting noise—the signal to his collaborators that food was there for the asking. A moment later there came crawling from every direction reptiles whose presence in the neighbourhood I had not even suspected. And now the meal began. One of the newcomers lay alongside the bird-catcher and caught hold of the part of the bird that was projecting from his jaws. Then they twisted in opposite directions, and the bird was broken in two. Others joined in, and so it went on until the bird was divided into suitably small portions, whereupon each gulped down his share of the feast. Every single alligator seemed to get a morsel—not a very big one, admittedly, but it is surprising how little food the enormous creatures seem to require.

Early in July the female begins building her nest on the bank of a suitable reach of swampy water. Consisting as it does of jumbled up twigs, brushwood and dead leaves, it looks almost like a pile raked together for a bonfire. In this she lays anything from one to two dozen eggs, which are incubated by the heat that accompanies the process of fermentation in the decaying vegetable matter. The incubation period is sixty-eight days, but the duration of the maternal instinct is much shorter than that, and it is only for the first two or three weeks after laying the eggs that the female watches over the nest. During that period it is advisable to approach only with great caution. If you come too close, the female will issue a warning by crawling slowly forward with open jaws. If you choose to ignore that warning, she will hurl herself at you like lightning—much faster than a man can move. Then she will break off the attack after five or six yards, and lie still again, jaws agape.

After three weeks or so the mother alligator forgets about the nest and the eggs in it, and when the youngsters finally crawl out of their shells they have to manage without any assistance. They are six to eight inches long at birth, black, with about twenty yellow rings round the body. They are only two or three days old when they start hunting for themselves and live for preference on small fry and frog spawn, otherwise on anything they can get their teeth into. Rotten or fresh, it is all the same to them, for they are natural carrion-eaters.

The young are greedy and bad-tempered, and though they live together they often go for one another—and then it is a struggle for dear life. They have no friends, only enemies. While they are small they keep to the shallow pools, where they frequently fall victim to predators hunting in the swamps, or to wading birds that will as cheerfully gobble up a young alligator as a frog. If they come too close to their own adult kith and kin the same thing happens, for the alligator is also a cannibal.

The teeth are hollow, and break off comparatively easily. There is always a new tooth underneath the old one, which quickly grows to the right size. This renovation process continues throughout the alligator's life. The jaws are prodigiously strong, and a full-grown alligator can easily break the bones of quite big land animals. Strangely enough, this strength operates only one way, being located in the group of muscles that closes the jaw; and in Buena Park in California I have often seen the keeper holding a gigantic alligator's jaw shut with one hand. It is not a method to be recommended to amateurs, however, since the alligator can, if he wants, break the grip by a rapid sideways rolling movement.

It is often said that the alligator kills with his tail, but this is only partly true. There is no doubt that he is capable of injuring quite large animals with a blow of his powerful tail, but he prefers to attack with his head and jaws. Like all saurians, the alligator can strike with his head at incredible speed, but only sideways. With this flip of his head, a full-grown alligator can break the leg of a horse. The heavy body and short, weak legs prevent him from moving forwards with anything like the same speed. His normal practice consists of a short run-up and a powerful forward lunge of the body—after which he flops on his belly.

The difference between the alligator and the other species of crocodile is very small. The crocodile is found in virtually all tropical areas, but the alligator only in the southeastern United States and in certain parts of China, while the caiman is widely distributed over Central and South America. The main difference in appearance is in the shape of the head. The crocodile's is triangular, with a pointed snout, the alligator's much more rounded, with a broader, blunter snout, and the caiman's somewhere between the two. In all of them it is the upper jaw that moves, and the tongue is firmly fixed to the lower jaw for its entire length.

Their dispositions vary considerably. Some species are good-humoured and easy to tame, while others are uncompromisingly wild and hostile. The fiercest of all is the Indian salt-water crocodile, which has killed more human beings than all the others put together. Crocodiles kill their victim by holding him under the water until he drowns. Then they combine to tear him in pieces, or anchor him to the bottom and wait for decomposition to set in.

There is no recorded and proven instance of American alligators attacking a man. They are easy to tame, and will then answer to their names. The tame alligator will open his jaws on command, and allow his keeper to put a piece of meat right down inside his throat without attempting to bite. His equable temperament makes him an admirable film extra, and all the 'crocodiles' in the innumerable Tarzan films have been American alligators.

The world's biggest collection of lizards and other reptiles is housed in the California Alligator Farm in Buena Park outside Los Angeles. The farm was established in 1908, essentially as a zoological park specializing in reptiles, but over the years it has enlarged its scope, and its daily programme now includes numerous other attractions. Among other things the public can be present at the feeding and taming of alligators and crocodiles. The tamed animals are hired out to film companies and other interested parties. Today the farm houses well over two thousand alligators.

The alligator, once on the point of extinction in America, now enjoys complete protection. Alligator-breeding for the sake of the skin is unknown, because the expense of feeding the beasts until they are big enough for their skins to have any commercial value would be prohibitive. The main purpose of the Buena Park farm therefore is to provide the film industry and the world's zoos with giant saurians of every kind.

Whether we fear them or not, their appearance is unquestionably striking. As they waddle along on their short, awkwardly straddling legs, with the upper part of the body raised off the ground, they look like prehistoric monsters. Which is exactly what they are—the direct descendants of the gigantic saurians which are lost in the mists of prehistory.

THIRTEEN

THE FOREST CLOWN

The young wife was bustling about in the kitchen one fine spring day, when she happened to glance out of the window into the garden, and went rigid with terror: her three-year-old son was playing happily with an enormous black bear some fifteen or twenty times his weight. To her amazement the pair of them seemed to be getting along excellently, until something irritated the boy—whereupon he seized a fish that his mother had left lying in a tub outside and gave the bear a good hard slap over the snout with it. Now, surely, the bear would savage the child. She stood there as if mesmerized, trying desperately to think of something she could do to save him. At that moment she heard her husband at the front door, and began yelling for help.

But her husband—who, unlike herself, had been born and bred in the place—took the whole thing completely calmly. If she disapproved of their son's playmate, all she had to do was go to the door and call him in. Somewhat reluctantly, she did so. Into the kitchen toddled the boy; and into the kitchen, behind him, shuffled the bear. Wild female screams put the latter to flight—not a little surprised, and indeed offended, by this deplorable lack of hospitality.

This happened in the little town of Banff in the Banff National Park, where animal life of every kind is protected all the year round. The population of two thousand has thus had to get used to sharing its streets and even its private gardens with wild animals such as the bear, moose, stag and roe deer. In all the years that I can remember, there has been no serious trouble between these animals and the regular inhabitants.

During my many years in Canada I have had countless experiences with bears. Some have been exciting, others amusing; not one has been dangerous. I have probably forgotten as many incidents as I have remembered. But one which I shall never forget, and which is as vivid to me today

as it was at the time, was my first encounter with a bear outside a zoo—in his natural habitat.

I was spending the summer in the forests of northern
Ontario, where I had undertaken to mark out the route for
a power line from an outpost farther south to a new power
station on the Ottawa. I had with me a small axe which I
used for marking the trees and cutting my way through the
undergrowth when it was particularly dense. Since the line
had to go straight through the forest, I was unable to avoid
the difficult places, and in the course of a day I got through
a lot of climbing and crawling.

At one point the forest was less dense than usual. The
terrain was mountainous, with not much roothold for large
trees. I found my path through a crevice barred by a great
spruce that had been upended in a gale, and was obliged to
climb over the roots, which, with the earth and moss cling-
ing to them, were the size of a barn door. I stuck my axe
in my belt and clambered up on top, let myself down to
arm's length on the other side, and jumped. I turned round
—and got the fright of my life.

Facing me, at a distance of a yard or less, stood the largest
bear I have ever seen. He was standing right up on his hind
legs, with his huge front paws stretched halfway towards
me. How big he really was, I hardly know today, because
over the years he has undoubtedly grown in my imagination,
but one thing is certain: he towered over me—and I stand
six feet five inches in my socks.

The first five seconds seemed like five eternities. Then I
panicked, turned and tried to climb up the vertical tree-
root that cut off my retreat. It was hopeless, as I doubtless
realized quite soon, however long-drawn-out the agony
may have seemed. Every second I expected to feel the enormous crooked claws in my back; but nothing happened.
Finally I drew out the axe from my belt and turned round,
determined to fight to the death.

But the bear had vanished. All I saw of him was his back-
side as he disappeared down the escarpment at full gallop.
Poor old Bruin had received as bad a fright as I had, and
each of us had decided at the same moment to show a clean
pair of heels—the only difference being that he had suc-

ceeded. From that day onward I have never been afraid of a bear.

Since then I have come to know the bear better than most, and I have yet to discover a single unpleasant trait in his character. On the little ranch we had for a time on the edge of the Clearwater forest reserve in Alberta, we had bears as daily visitors for the warm half of the year. They used to go down into the pasture and graze with our horses, and they would drop into the farm to see if there were any sweets we wanted to get rid of. I have seen my wife sit down and feed a cub from her hand, while the mother grazed peacefully a few feet away. That, it's true, always made me slightly nervous, for in general it is extremely dangerous. On occasions when I have wanted to get the right camera angle, I myself have come between the mother and her cubs—which is even more dangerous. But nothing ever happened, and I believe this was simply because they were used to us and paid us the compliment of trusting us. It is true, of course, that bears have been known to maim or kill human beings and attack livestock. But these are exceptional cases, and there is always a good explanation.

The black bear and the brown bear are both vegetarians, with teeth that are characteristic of herbivorous animals, though there are also the rudiments of carnivorous teeth. The only carnivorous bears to be found today on dry land are the North American grizzly and his cousin from Alaska, the kodiak bear. But even these two live on vegetable food as much as on meat. The only member of the bear family that lives exclusively on meat is the polar bear, the reason being that there is no vegetation to be found in his principal haunts.

Although most bears are herbivorous, when they are half-starved they have been known to kill a sheep or a calf. This happens only when they are too close to civilization—when man intrudes in nature and deprives them of their normal means of subsistence, either by appropriating it to his own use or by a policy of extermination. An example is the Norwegian cloudberry bogs, which are one of the bear's natural sources of food, and which in recent years have been stripped completely so that not even the unripe berries are allowed to remain.

I have known several instances of people being maimed by bears. But however much I sympathize with the people concerned, it is only fair to say that in almost every instance they asked for trouble. Every year the national parks of North America provide examples, even though there are stringent rules about going too close to bears. People forget that for all their charming and amusing ways they are not pets. The bear sits up by the side of the road and begs, and people throw food. Then they get out to take a photograph, and the bear does them no harm. But the photographer wants some close-ups. He comes between a mother bear and her young—and that's that.

The most vivid example of this kind of stupidity that I remember occurred in Banff itself. A young American honeymoon couple stopped to photograph a bear who was begging for sweets from every car that passed. The bear duly came up to their car and was fed. It even took a biscuit from the man's hand, neatly and cleanly, without so much as brushing his fingers. Then the man had the idea of getting his wife to photograph the bear taking a piece of chocolate from his mouth. He put the chocolate between his teeth and leant out of the window. But as the bear's gaping jaw approached his face he had second thoughts and began to withdraw his head. The bear lunged out with his front paw to rescue the chocolate which was now on the point of disappearing—and that was the end of *that* story: the sharp claws sank into the man's ear and removed half his face.

Or rather, that was not the end of the story. The end came later. The injured man was raced to hospital and his life saved. Plastic surgery even gave him a new face. But the unfortunate bear was pursued by the park-keeper and shot. He had 'attacked' a man, and in park law that means the death sentence. The only tear shed for *him* came from the park-keeper who had been obliged to act as executioner; he knew that this particular bear was one of the best-natured in the whole park, and that never in his life had he wittingly injured a mouse, let alone a man.

The bear is good-humoured, playful, and a natural

clown. He will think up the most incredible tricks to induce people to throw him food, and he is intelligent enough to understand what they fall for most easily. The only time the bear may be directly dangerous is the rutting season—and he is hardly unique in this. I don't believe there is a single authenticated case of a bear attacking a human being unless he felt his life was in danger, or unless there was some misunderstanding such as the one I have described.

This is just as true of the grizzly as it is of the brown or black bear. The grizzly is shy and gives man a wide berth, but if pressed too hard he won't hesitate to attack. I have seen a grizzly go for three hunters who had hemmed him in so that escape was impossible. He came on like an express train, and the well-aimed shots that the hunters kept pumping into his body seemed to have no effect whatsoever. Two of the hunters sought refuge in a tree, but the third went on firing until his magazine was empty. The last shot, fired at a range of fifteen to twenty yards, broke the bear's spine and paralysed his hind legs. But he continued steadily forward towards his tormentor on his front legs alone, with his hind legs trailing behind.

The third hunter dropped his rifle and began climbing the tree he was standing under. He was only in the nick of time. With his last remaining strength the bear aimed a blow that hit the tree a few inches below the man's foot and tore a broad strip of bark and wood from the trunk. He tried to rise, but it was beyond his power. With a final tremendous effort he fell on the rifle lying at the foot of the tree and smashed it to smithereens. Then he lay still in death.

It was found that twelve of the shots had hit the bear, and that at least four of them were mortal: two in the brain, one in the heart and one in the spine. It was will-power alone that had kept him going. This peaceful giant, who had never attacked man or his property, had to die just to enable a 'sportsman' to boast of his bravery and skill in bringing down such a dangerous beast of prey.

Whenever a farmer loses a sheep or a calf, it tends to be a bear who gets the blame—even if only one in a thousand has ever tasted meat. In 99 per cent of those cases in which a proper investigation has been made, the accusations against the bear have proved to be without foundation. But when livestock are lost through inadequate supervision it is convenient to have a scapegoat—and who more suitable than Bruin, whom very few people have ever seen outside a cage in a zoo?

What is most interesting of all, however, is the loud-mouthed bear-hunters who are hero-worshipped for having brought down so and so many bears. Some heroism! It would take an exceptionally poor shot to fail to hit this large, amiable creature at a range of a hundred yards or more; and since the bear will neither attack unless provoked nor, as a rule, be in any great hurry to remove himself, it requires neither courage nor cunning to pick him off. There is as much heroism in shooting a bear as there is in cutting off the head of a chicken.

FOURTEEN   THE INCOMPARABLE
                            WOLVERINE

'If a wolverine appears in the trapper's vicinity, there are only two alternatives. The trapper must either get rid of the wolverine at the first opportunity, or pack his bags and move on.'

These words occur in a handbook for trappers that is found in every hunting outpost in the Canadian north, where for many people the capture of valuable fur-bearing animals is still the main means of livelihood. And I have to add that it usually ends with the trapper taking the easy way out, gathering up his traps and other paraphernalia and putting as many miles as he can between the wolverine and himself; for he very rarely manages to conquer this little tyrant when once the latter has decided to make life hell for him.

What causes the wolverine to conceive a hatred for certain trappers is mysterious. The fact remains that I have hardly ever heard of anyone else being molested by him. He is quite indifferent to lumberjacks and others who venture into the forests and plains, but trappers infuriate him. Perhaps he regards them as sworn enemies of all animal life, and makes it his object to avenge all the injury they have done to the forest-dwellers in his zone of interest.

The wolverine is not one of the biggest beasts of prey. A full-grown animal weighs no more than forty-five to fifty-five pounds and is no bigger than a good-sized fox, but is very powerfully built; pound for pound he is perhaps the strongest beast of prey in existence. He is exceptionally intelligent and quite fearless. When he finds it necessary to fight for his rights, he will take on allcomers, even a grizzly bear. And generally both the bear and the wolf maintain a respectful distance from him.

I have lived in wolverine country in various parts of northern Canada, and have had the opportunity of studying him at close quarters. From personal observation I find myself unable to accept many of the theories that have been put forward about his bloodlust and destructiveness.

There is an ancient Amerindian superstition according to which the wolverine is the Devil incarnate—it being beyond their comprehension that any ordinary, mortal animal could possess so much cunning and impudence. Traces of this superstition still survive among the Indians, and they treat the wolverine with a mixture of deference and fear. I cannot agree with my Indian friends; and in many respects, I find him deserving of sympathy and admiration. He lives in a hard and brutal world, and he puts his gifts to excellent use to protect himself and his family. It isn't malice, but a form of self-defence, that motivates his destructive urge.

When a wolverine sets out to drive away a trapper, he makes a thorough job of it. A few winters ago, when I was living in northern Ontario, a trapper I knew fell foul of one and was totally ruined. He had had an excellent season, and had chalked up an impressive score of furs—mostly valuable skins such as marten, otter, mink and fox. As the season was drawing to an end, disaster struck: a wolverine entered his hunting territory.

All hunting for furs is done by trapping so that the skin remains intact. It is a time-honoured method, though a crude and brutal one which inflicts long-drawn-out physical and mental pain on the animals. The trapper selects an area, the so-called trapline, and applies to the authorities for a monopoly within it; conflict between two men hunting the same area is thus prevented. As soon as the first snow has fallen, the trapper goes out and sets his traps. The areas involved are by no means small, but as far as possible he inspects every trap once a day and collects the animals that have been caught during the night.

On the day that marked the beginning of the end, the trapper in question put on his snowshoes as usual and set out in the grey light of dawn. Near the first trap he was perturbed to see fresh wolverine tracks. When he reached the trap his fear was fully confirmed: the wolverine had already been there. The trap had held a marten, but all

that remained was a few tattered bits of skin. The steel trap itself was a total wreck. In growing dismay he followed his regular route, and every time he came to a trap it was the same story: if an animal had been in it, the animal had been torn to shreds and the trap destroyed or removed.

Wherever he could, he restored his traps to some sort of working order; then he drew on his reserve store to complete the trapline. But the very next day the heartbreaking experience was repeated: the wolverine had visited every single trap, and the destruction was complete.

Clearly it was war to the death, for the trapper had no intention of being driven out of his territory without a fight. Systematically he ran over the various ways he might get rid of his tormentor. It was a bleak and depressing prospect. Basically there were three possible methods, of which two seemed doomed from the outset. Putting out poisoned food would have been a waste of time and meat, for no wolverine would go near such bait—least of all one that had fresh meat from the traps on his daily menu. Trying to catch the wolverine in a steel trap was equally hopeless, for even if, against all the odds, the animal were to get caught, no trap would be strong enough to hold him. This trapper had seen with his own eyes how a wolverine had broken through a bear-trap which normally took two men to open it.

The only hope, then, was to follow the wolverine's tracks until he caught sight of him, and then to get close enough to down him with a well-aimed shot. But this was no small task either, since he could safely assume that the wolverine was also aware of the possibility, and would therefore take particular care to remain out of sight.

At crack of dawn the trapper set out, and it wasn't long before he came upon very recent wolverine tracks in the snow. All day long he followed them. When daylight gradually began to fade, he was many miles from his log cabin, and he realized that he would have to spend the night away from home.

This in itself was no problem, because like all trappers he was well prepared for such an eventuality. Right at the end of his trapline he had what is known as a cache: a well-stocked storeroom and a bunk for the night. This place was less than a mile away, and he set off straight away in order to get there before it became completely dark. He was looking forward to a comfortable night in his little refuge, where he had ample supplies of food, blankets, firewood and matches. There was even a spare rifle and ammunition, carefully wrapped in oilpaper.

The cache lay in a natural hollow under a mountain spur, and the approach was well protected with stout logs and a number of large stones which, with much effort and exertion, he had piled up to keep out wild animals. But he had reckoned without his tormentor—the wolverine had already been there. The entrance to the hollow, which the hunter had felt confident not even a bear could force, had been child's play for the wolverine. The stones had been rolled away. The logs lay strewn about.

The hollow itself was a sorry sight. The blankets had been torn into shreds, the tins of food ground to bits, the flourbag slashed open and the flour spilt all over the hollow. The rifle had gone; so had the matchboxes, which had been wrapped in oilpaper. The destruction was final and complete.

It was a long, cold night for the trapper. But everything comes to an end; and next morning he went back to the cabin, where he began preparations for a new attack. On his way home he had shot a roe, and from this he cut a large juicy steak which he placed in the forest nearby. Then he rigged up a rifle in a tree and aimed it at the bait. Finally, he made a kind of spring-gun, using a length of string: when the wolverine took the meat, it would jerk tight and pull the trigger. The string he covered carefully with snow.

When everything was ready, he retreated to the cabin, put out the light, and sat down by the window to wait. Out there between the trees he could just glimpse the bait in the moonlight.

He may have dozed off for a while, but suddenly he started up, very wide awake. He could make out a form standing by the meat—and he was certain that the form was that of the wolverine. But he had heard no shot, and now, as his eyes got used to the darkness, he could see that the wolverine was on the point of making off with the bait. Something had gone wrong. He grabbed his rifle, dashed out of the door, and bounded out into the snow. He reached the place just as the wolverine, with the fresh deer-steak between his jaws, was preparing to disappear into the forest.

The wolverine dropped the meat, drew back a step or two, and bared his teeth. For two days he had had nothing to eat: the traps had not been set, and he himself had been too busy playing cat and mouse with the trapper to have any time for hunting. He was tired and hungry, his dinner lay in front of him, and no power on earth was going to take it away. He was prepared to fight to the last drop of blood.

The trapper took aim—he had not expected it to be as easy as this—but when he pressed the trigger nothing happened. And suddenly he realized that, in his haste, of the three rifles hanging on the wall of the cabin he had snatched the only one that was out of order. But this time the forest devil was not going to get away with it. Lifting the rifle above his head, he sprang forward—he could still use the butt as a club, however flimsy a weapon it might be against a wolverine.

It is difficult to know what would have happened if at this point destiny had not lent a hand. When the trapper, carried away by rage, threw himself on the wolverine, he completely forgot the spring-gun. There had been nothing wrong with it; but when the wolverine had found the bait, from long habit he had investigated it thoroughly before trying to remove it. He had discovered the string fastened to the meat, and even if he couldn't see its significance, it was clear to him that it spelled danger in one form or another. He had seen too many traps in his life to dream of trying to remove a bait that was fastened in any way. He dug cautiously in the surrounding snow—but could find no trap there. The danger, therefore, must lie at the other end of the string.

This was something beyond the wolverine's comprehension but, being a cautious fellow, he had made up his mind not to help himself to anything that might bring retribution without a careful investigation first. He had followed the string over to the trees where the rifle was fastened, and had instinctively understood that that was where the danger lay. Then he had gone back to the bait and started gnawing at the thread, taking great care all the time not to tug or jerk it.

The trapper had been standing with one foot on the end of the string, and as he hurled himself at the wolverine he kicked out with his other foot, thereby giving it a powerful tug. A shot rang out—and the trapper fell to the ground in the snow with a bullet in his hip. The wolverine snatched up the meat and vanished immediately into the forest.

Late next day, half dead from exhaustion and loss of blood, the trapper arrived at the nearest trading post, where he was treated. A day or two later the storekeeper set out into the forest with two Indians to collect all the furs that the trapper had accumulated during the winter. They might have saved themselves the trouble. The shed containing the furs had been broken into, and every single skin had been ripped and gnawed to pieces. The door of the log cabin stood open, and the interior looked as if it had been hit by a tornado. Everything capable of being destroyed had been destroyed. The forest devil had had the last word.

I need hardly add that the trapper never returned to the area.

After that story you may well wonder at my continuing to feel sympathy for the wolverine. But there is another side to the picture. Looked at another way, it was the man who had trespassed on the wolverine's preserves and caused a disturbance in the natural order. For the wolverine, there were only two possibilities: to protect what he regarded as his property, or to leave the place he knew and try his luck in fresh fields. Naturally, he chose the first.

Although the wolverine looks like a diminutive bear, he is actually a member of the marten family, and it may be this that has given rise to the rumours of his insatiable bloodlust. There have certainly been instances of his spreading death and destruction among a flock of sheep, but normally he keeps as far from civilization as he can, and he is one of the beasts of prey that is most rarely seen or studied.

As a rule he hunts alone, living mostly on small animals

that are not too difficult for him to catch. Given the opportunity, he is more than ready to attack the larger hoofed
animals, such as elk, cariboo, reindeer or roe, but this
opportunity only arises if the animal is sick or injured; for
the wolverine is not particularly quick in his movements,
and cannot compete with the ungulates in speed. They in
turn have no particular fear of him; they know that they
needn't worry as long as they don't allow him to get too
near. Thus the wolverine's life depends on his ability to
catch his prey by cunning.

Every second autumn the wolverine seeks a mate, and
in the late spring produces two or three offspring. The family
remains together till late summer, when the father slouches
off in search of new adventures, leaving the mother to take
care of the young until they are big enough to fend for
themselves. Nor is it uncommon for the parents to come
together again after their offspring have gone their several
ways.

The wolverine has to live a hard and pitiless life in wild
forest and mountain areas, and he is always ready to fight
for his existence. The urge to destroy may well be there,
but it is directed only against those who intrude into and
disturb that part of nature which he regards as his by right.

Heroic courage and a hot temper are not exactly the
characteristics we tend to associate with rabbits. Nor do
many of us rate their intelligence particularly high. But
then most of us are given to underestimating and misunderstanding animals to a grotesque extent—until we
really get to know them. Before I became acquainted with
Bibi, I had seldom thought of rabbits except as things to
put in a pot. After two and a half years of life with him I
feel a deep respect for rabbits, though I'm aware that not all
rabbits are quite like Bibi.

My remarkable life with Bibi began one Easter in Canada.
My wife was visiting a shop where they sold baby rabbits,
'Easter bunnies', which parents used to buy and take home
for their children. Among the few left over at the end of the
sale, my wife noticed a little coal-black fellow sitting
timidly in a corner, while the others pranced happily about.
He was not much bigger than a mouse, and his ears were
hardly larger than my thumbnail. The shopkeeper told my
wife that nobody wanted him because he looked so miser-
able and lifeless. The inevitable result was that she felt so
sorry for him that she had to bring him home.

Of course there could be no question of putting such a
helpless little creature in a cage, so he was allowed to live
in the house. The first obstacle to overcome was his introduction to the animal we already had: the cat Fluffy.

This went better than we had dared hope. Fluffy studied
the newcomer attentively for a while; then he stretched out
a paw and touched Bibi gently—knocking him head over
heels. Fluffy evidently concluded that the poor little thing
needed a protector, and from that moment assumed the
role himself. Mucho, the dog we acquired soon after, also
fell for Bibi from the start, and very soon the three of them
were inseparable.

Rabbits are in the habit of dropping their pellets

anywhere and everywhere, and this, of course, we were not prepared to tolerate. If Bibi was going to live indoors, he would have to be house-trained. So he was given his own little sand-box out in the passage, and there he was expected to go when nature called. It was astonishing how soon he learned what was required; and for this, I am sure, we had Fluffy to thank. Fluffy, who couldn't endure dirty habits, kept a sharp eye on Bibi; and if Bibi forgot himself there was trouble.

I had always supposed that rabbits have enormous ears from the moment they are born, or at least that the ears grow in proportion with their bodies. This may be so in some cases, but with Bibi it was very different. He grew bigger and bigger, while his ears seemed to be holding themselves in check, until at last they suddenly began to grow, almost as an afterthought, and finished by becoming the most beautiful pair of rabbit's ears one could wish.

It soon became clear that Fluffy was Bibi's idol: what Fluffy did, Bibi had to do. Fluffy had always been allowed to sit on a high kitchen chair and eat breakfast with us, and Bibi naturally demanded the same privilege. A stranger would have been amazed to come unexpectedly into our dining-room and find us assembled at the breakfast table: my wife, myself, a cat and a rabbit, each with his or her own plate. Like Fluffy, Bibi had impeccable table manners, sitting on his chair and eating without ever making a mess. But he gradually developed a peculiarity: he insisted on being served exactly the same food as my wife, whether it was meat, fowl, fish or fruit. Indeed he seemed to prefer a leg of chicken to a carrot.

He was very fond of cakes, too, and was always the first to arrive when my wife had been baking. Perhaps he understood that the red light on the kitchen range meant that something was happening in the oven. At any rate, when a cake was baking he would come hopping in from time to time through the garden door, take a look at the range—and sit down and wait.

Bibi soon fell into a kind of daily routine which he maintained throughout the period of growing up. At six o'clock in the morning he would begin to play with Fluffy.

The game consisted of their creeping up on each other by turns, and then chasing each other through every room in the house. They would keep this up for an hour; then they would race to my wife's bed. There the cat had his regular place at her feet, the whole bottom half of the bed being out of bounds to Bibi. Bibi therefore chose a position up on the pillow, where he settled himself comfortably on his hind legs and began his morning toilet. First he washed his face; then he polished his ears, one at a time, licking his front paws and rubbing the whole length of his ears between them until they gleamed in the morning sun. It was like watching a woman doing her hair in front of the mirror.

When we acquired Mucho, Bibi spent most of the day with him out in the garden. They had many different games, but the most amusing of them all consisted of Bibi riding around on Mucho's back. Possibly they got the idea from one of the cowboy films on television; or they may have hit on it by chance. Anyway, Bibi's rides were an almost daily occurrence. Mucho would lie down on the grass while Bibi clambered up on his back and held on tight. Then Mucho would start running round and round the lawn. Faster and faster they went—and the game invariably ended in the same way: when Mucho reached a certain speed, one of his sharper turns would send Bibi hurtling through the air on to the grass.

It sometimes happened, during our play in the garden, that I would tease Bibi a little too much. Since he had a hot temper he would at times get angry with me, and then he didn't hesitate to attack me—and bite. If I had a newspaper or something similar in my hand, I could always keep him at bay, as he soon came to realize. However, he also had a secret weapon with which I became acquainted in a singularly unpleasant way. He would charge in, and when he was a yard or so away perform a somersault on his front legs, so that he had his hind-quarters towards me. Right in the middle of the somersault he would aim a jet of evil-smelling fluid at me, with devastating accuracy. After two such attacks, whenever it was clear that he didn't want me around I kept my distance.

Bibi's sporadic hostility towards me may have stemmed

from the pranks I sometimes played on him, or it may have originated in a shock I once gave him, entirely innocently, when he was still quite small, and which he may have remembered on every subsequent occasion that we fell out. I had been sitting at my ease one day with a cup of coffee and a cigarette while I read the paper, and Bibi came hopping up to investigate more closely. It was probably the first time he had noticed this curious object that sent a column of smoke curling up to the ceiling. Always inquisitive, he felt he ought to look into the matter, and he stuck his nose straight into the glowing cigarette. He may have singed himself a little, but the worst of it was that he got his nostrils full of smoke. He let out the most heart-rending wail, and began coughing and sneezing. I'm not certain which of us was the more startled, but from that day on, I'm sure, Bibi always regarded me with a certain mistrust.

Bibi knew his name, and always came when called, even if he was out touring the neighbourhood. It was remarkable also that he seemed to be able to distinguish the sound of our car from other people's. If my wife was out in the car, I had only to watch Bibi to know when to expect her. As soon as she was near he would run to the door and sit up on his hind legs to welcome her home. And he never made a mistake.

When Bibi was just over two years old, my wife decided that he ought to have the companionship of his own kind— perhaps a mate. We weren't too keen to fill the whole house with rabbits, so we had to find some other solution. There was a local zoo where they had just established a section for children, in which they had the usual domestic animals. These animals seemed to enjoy excellent conditions, so we decided to take Bibi there to see if he would like to join his fellow rabbits.

The attempt was a dismal failure, perhaps because Bibi had got into strange ways for a rabbit. On the very first day he got into terrible trouble, when he started paying court to all the females. The other males took a very poor view of this upstart trying to take command of the harem before he had even been introduced, and that evening they made a concerted attack on him. We should, of course, have taken this into our calculations, for both rabbits and hares are extremely intolerant of male strangers who push their way into an established family group. They often attack *en masse*, sometimes with fatal results for the intruder.

When we went to visit Bibi next day he was in a sorry plight. He had been so savagely bitten by the others that there wasn't a square inch of skin on his body that was free from sores. He lay by himself in a corner more dead than alive, and there seemed no alternative but to take him home again. It took two weeks of nursing and five penicillin injections before he recovered, and appreciably longer before he got back his old exuberance: clearly his misfortune had affected him psychologically as well as physically.

We realized that the time had come to find him a more suitable home, and it so happened that the son of a Norwegian farmer whom we knew had just lost his rabbit. We presented him with Bibi, and at the same time we bought a young, attractive female to keep him company in his new home in the country.

Bibi had a fine old time. And one Sunday when we were there on a visit Bibi was able to show us a litter of healthy, frisky young rabbits. The cup of happiness was full for Bibi and his friends, including ourselves. But it was the last time we saw him. On our next visit we learned of his dreadful fate.

The area had long been plagued by ownerless dogs who had gradually become wild. They hunted in packs, and our farmer friend had already suffered serious losses among his poultry, lambs and young calves. Late one afternoon five or six of these wild dogs had come surging on to the farm and made straight for the family of rabbits, who were jumping around in the yard.

It was then that Bibi showed his heroism. Sending the mother and her young scuttling for the shelter of the farmhouse, he turned and faced the entire pack. The farmer saw what was happening from a window, and came running to the door; but before he could do anything it was too late. Bibi was torn to pieces before his eyes—but the unfortunate rabbit had saved his family from certain death, and grief at his fate was to some extent assuaged by pride in his heroism.

As I said at the beginning, I am far from supposing that all rabbits are like Bibi, but I am sure that, given the opportunity, most of them would show many of the same characteristics. In any case, the courage of the proverbially timid rabbit is beyond doubt.

SIXTEEN

FLUFFY AND HIS COMPANIONS

Of all the animals, wild and tame, that I have had over the years, there is only one that I never succeeded in mastering —the domestic cat.

No creature on this earth can train a domestic cat. He acknowledges only one lord and master—himself—and only one will—his own. He is sublime in his disdain and his impudence. He can be intolerably condescending, and he has no respect for the feelings of others—he is egoism incarnate.

A household cat can be the very devil when he feels in the mood—and he can be an angel in animal's clothing when he really likes you and feels you've earned a little encouragement. He may consent to your stroking his back and scratching him behind the ears; he may even go to the length of inviting such attention by rubbing himself against your legs and purring. But he decides for himself how long this should go on, and he has no scruples about putting his claws in the hand that strokes him, if he feels that the overtures have gone on long enough.

People who think they are showing a cat who is master in the house by taking him by the scruff of the neck and throwing him out are making a great mistake. Such an action is a crushing moral defeat for them. The victor is always the cat, who has succeeded in upsetting his owner to such an extent as to make him resort to violence.

Nobody knows for certain when the cat decided to abandon his hard life out in the wild and become a household pet instead. It may have been at the time of the first Pharoahs, or even earlier. One can only suppose that he became tired of having to hunt, night after night, for emaciated fieldmice—when the neighbouring palace was flowing with milk and honey.

To begin with, he came and went as he pleased—as

indeed he has continued to do ever since. But he never ventured far afield, and was never away for long at a time, because he understood clearly that a good relationship has to be cultivated. He soon learned that milk and other items would be served if he did his hunting within the confines of the palace. Nothing suited him better, since it was precisely there that the fattest mice and rats were to be found. And so, in the course of time, this became a matter of habit— but he was never tamed and never gave up his freedom.

My best teacher in feline psychology was my wife's large Persian cat, Fluffy. He was not so very big when we acquired him at the age of six weeks, but it wasn't long before he began to assert himself in the house. Like most animals, he made a beeline for my wife, and for her he would do absolutely anything. Between these two a bond was formed that lasted through good days and bad for the whole of Fluffy's life. With me it was another story.

I don't know what Fluffy had against me, whether it was jealousy over my wife, or whether he was unable to make out what purpose I served in the house. In any case he came gradually to regard me as a kind of necessary evil, something he must manage to put up with until he could find some way of getting rid of me. And, like the intelligent and realistic creature that he was, he soon came to the conclusion that since he had to put up with me he might just as well exploit me for all I was worth.

Every day when I got home from the office, he was waiting for me with his plaything, which consisted of a piece of long-haired fur tied to the end of a string. I had to run around with this piece of fur dangling behind me, or swing it in the air, so that Fluffy could jump for it or hunt it. The playtime lasted half an hour every day, and I would never have dreamed of trying to get out of it.

During the game Fluffy would sit down and start washing his face. His toy was then totally ignored. But if I tried to sit down with the paper he was there in a flash with the string. *His* taking a rest in the game didn't mean that *I* could sit down and relax before the half-hour was up. It was no use hiding behind the paper and pretending not to see him,

118

because then he would climb up on the back of the chair behind me, and jump over my shoulder and clean through the paper. The toy lasted Fluffy for the whole of his life, and there weren't many days in all those years that he let me off the daily game—even though in time he cut down its duration considerably.

Another game I had to take part in every day was the little dance I was expected to perform with Fluffy lying on his back in my arms. He particularly enjoyed my version of an old-time polka. But once these two daily practices were over he would turn his back on me and spend the rest of the day wandering around as if I didn't exist.

It took five years before I gained Fluffy's confidence and friendship, but then it seemed as if he had determined to make up for lost time. To my mortification I became aware that, while in his younger days he had played with me because he enjoyed it, as he grew older he continued with the daily game to give *me* pleasure. He evidently thought that if I was so utterly childish as to insist on playing with the piece of fur, it was up to him to satisfy me.

Fluffy was in many ways a copycat, and his favourite subject for imitation was my wife. Whatever she was eating —grapes, oranges, apples—he wanted to have the same. He is the only cat I know of who would eat chocolate and caramels. He refused to have his food served in a bowl on the floor, like other cats: he wouldn't eat unless his food was served on the table, like ours. We had a kitchen chair rather like a bar-stool, and when Fluffy sat on it his head and shoulders came above the level of the table. This chair he annexed, and no one else was allowed to use it. Since he ate more frequently than we did, his bowl was always left standing on the corner of the kitchen table, and if he was hungry and the bowl was empty he would get up on the chair and miaow until someone came and served him.

When we acquired Fluffy we hadn't had any domestic animals for some time, but our intention was to fill the house again as soon as possible. It so happened that Fluffy's first playmate was the rabbit Bibi, and as I have already said, this relationship was an outstandingly successful one. However, it wasn't long before these two had a companion, whom I have also mentioned—the dog Mucho, who came from a broken home and was in dismally poor shape and spirits when we took pity on him. We were a little anxious about how this would work, but the first meeting between the three of them went off without incident.

At first Fluffy was somewhat reserved towards Mucho, though never unfriendly. Bibi, on the other hand, positively overflowed with friendliness. When the two of them were playing together, Fluffy would usually sit watching with supreme dignity; but he was still a very young cat, and from time to time he would let himself be drawn into the game. As long as this was played in accordance with Fluffy's rules all went well—and the other two soon learned Fluffy's rules and stuck to them.

Unfortunately we had Mucho for only a relatively short time. He was run over by a careless driver and died at the vet's. But his place was soon filled—this time by a very different kind of animal, which even Fluffy took some time to get used to. This was a four-month-old male African lion. He was the mascot of a local football club, and we acquired him when he suddenly became homeless. The club was still the owner, so we were merely foster-parents.

It is hard to know how Fluffy felt when he suddenly found this enormous jungle cat sharing his home, since he kept his feelings well hidden from view. Although Fluffy was an exceptionally large cat, he was tiny in comparison with Simba. Anyway he wasn't afraid of the lion; for the first few days it seemed rather to be the lion who was uneasy about him. Wherever Simba went, he found himself followed by Fluffy's hypnotic, staring eyes, which never blinked and never left him.

None the less, there was a certain unmistakable wariness on the cat's side, until one day something happened that caused him to lose much of the respect he must have felt for the lion, something that convinced Fluffy once and for all that he was much smarter than the king of beasts.

We were all in the living-room one afternoon, and Simba had for the first time plucked up the courage to jump up on the sofa, where he sat quietly and peacefully looking round him. On the wall directly opposite the sofa was a fireplace, which we had had framed with black polished flagstones. All of a sudden Simba jumped up as if someone had put a rocket under him. For a moment he remained staring fixedly ahead; then he leaped to the ground and resumed his staring. His tail began to swing to and fro—and then, with a growl that made the coffee-cups rattle, he went into the attack. The whole thing had happened so quickly that it took us some seconds to realize what had produced this violent reaction. Simba galloped straight for the fireplace and with an enormous leap hurled himself with outstretched fore-paws right against the polished flagstones—whereupon he rolled over and over with a most foolish expression on his face.

From the sofa he had seen his own reflection in the flagstones, and had assumed that another lion had forced his way into the house. It was bad enough finding himself surrounded by cat, dog and rabbit, without a rival lion turning up and contending with him for precedence. There was only one thing to do, and that was to show this intruder who was lord and master. No sooner thought than done.

It is possible that when he had launched his attack Simba had not really intended any harm, that he merely wanted to give the stranger a box or two on the ears to let him know who was in charge. But the other had had the impertinence to give him a punch on the nose which had nearly knocked him out. And now fury seized him.

A little unsteadily he got to his feet again, all the time keeping his eye on his reflection. He observed how the other lion imitated all his movements, and was highly irritated. Simba growled again. Then he crept a little nearer—and let fly a hook. The other lion did exactly the same, and their paws collided so heavily that Simba felt the pain right up to his shoulder. His fury grew, and he hit out at his reflection again and again, until suddenly it dawned on him that something was wrong. Cautiously he felt the cold stone with his paw—and then the truth became clear. The coward he was fighting was sheltering on the other side of the fireplace.

Now followed a few minutes of shadow-boxing, as

Simba time and again swerved into the fireplace from the side in order to take his enemy in the rear. When this failed he tried using his claws to tear the flagstones from the wall, with the same negative result. Finally he gave up, turned his back on his reflection and shuffled away into a corner where he could lie without seeing the accursed fireplace.

Fluffy had followed the incident with the greatest interest, and if a cat is capable of feeling amused I am sure he was. *Schadenfreude* was written all over his face—*he* had long been aware that the nonsense in the fireplace was a mirror image of himself. But one thing had impressed Fluffy and everyone else present, including Simba, and that was the lion's roar. This was the first time it had been heard, and it was a formidable noise. For Simba it was a discovery of the greatest importance—he had found his voice and become an adult at one and the same moment.

Until then Simba's favourite amusement had been to steal Fluffy's milk—from right under his nose; but now this game was finished. The next time he tried it Fluffy went right up to him and gave him a powerful smack on the snout, and Simba was so taken aback that he never tried that game again.

As time went on, our animal family continued to grow, even though individual members of it dropped out. When Bibi was sent away to the country we got a new dog, the tiny elkhound puppy whom we christened Bamse. He and Fluffy at once became friends, even though Fluffy, as usual, made it quite clear who was lord and master in the house. Bamse could never do enough for the cat, while Fluffy, in his characteristic manner, often treated him with condescension and disdain.

But their friendship was beyond question, and when Fluffy was in trouble he never hesitated to summon Bamse. In spite of his size Fluffy was no fighter, and this may be connected with the fact that he was neuter. He was brave enough when he sat at home on his own steps; then he was ready to take on any cat in the neighbourhood, because he knew that Bamse was close at hand and keeping an eye on him. But outside our property he sometimes got into deep waters—there were two big neighbouring toms in particular who liked to go for him—and it was then that he screamed for help. And Bamse never failed him.

We have always felt that there ought to be two dogs in a family, since this is of great psychological value for the animals. So it was not long after acquiring Bamse that we bought his brother Bimbo, who was also accepted without hesitation by Fluffy. But this happy *ménage à trois* was short-lived, for one day when Bimbo had ventured out alone he was stolen, and in spite of persistent police inquiries was never found. Bamse was badly upset by the loss, and when soon afterwards we were offered four baby rabbits we took them as playmates for him. We remembered, of course, the excellent relationship between Bibi and Mucho.

But now Fluffy revealed a character trait of which until then we had been unaware. He was jealous. Fundamentally he had nothing against the rabbits, and indeed he and Bibi, as we have seen, had been the best of friends. While the new rabbits were little he showed the same interest in them that he had shown in Bibi; but as time went by his attitude changed.

For they were Bamse's rabbits, and Bamse took this responsibility very seriously. He would spend the whole day out in the garden with them, keeping watch over them, trotting after them wherever they went, and making sure that they didn't go too near the garden fence. Beyond this fence lurked every kind of danger in the form of neighbouring dogs and cats, and Bamse knew how untrustworthy these were. Bamse also possessed an unusually strong sense of order, and he felt that the four rabbits ought always to keep together in a compact little group. When they wanted to jump, they ought all, in his view, to jump in the same direction and at the same speed. But the rabbits lacked this sense of order, and when they jumped they invariably did so in four different directions. And so Bamse had constantly to be gathering them up into a little group again.

And throughout the day, whenever Bamse had managed to assemble three rabbits in a group, and made a breathless arrival with the fourth, the other three set off again in three different directions. Never in all his life had Bamse worked so hard, and when the evening came and the rabbits were settled in their cage for the night he was flat out and ready for sleep. He was too tired to have anything much to do with Fluffy—who gradually developed a distinct grievance against the rabbits, whom he considered responsible for Bamse's lack of attention.

This was the only time we had any friction within the family, and when after seven or eight months the rabbits were sent out to the ranch, the matter was sorted out between the two of them and forgotten.

Then Lady entered their lives, and again the newcomer was accepted by Fluffy. Lady was an exceptionally beautiful border collie, but she was a wreck of an animal when we first brought her home. We had found her in the police kennel for ownerless dogs, and as she was sick she was to have been put to death the next day. We took her home and sent for the best vet in town, who after examining her told us that there was no hope. My wife nursed Lady for a month before she was well enough to be declared out of danger—but it was nearly a year before she was completely fit again.

Throughout this period Bamse and Fluffy were full of concern and sympathy. They seemed to understand that Lady was sick and in need of help, and Bamse continued to take care of her, Fluffy's feeling for her began to cool somewhat, though his jealousy was less in evidence than it had been with the rabbits. Anyway, it became clear that anyone who made too many claims on Bamse could expect the cold shoulder from Fluffy.

About the time that Lady regained her health we acquired the skunk Sniffy, whose ways I have already described. Again we had an animal of a completely different species, and again he was accepted by Fluffy without reservation. To begin with, until Sniffy had learned to behave properly in the house, he was liable to receive punishment at Fluffy's hand. But whenever Fluffy gave him a smack on the nose he took care that his claws never protruded or hurt the little skunk.

When Lady produced a litter of eight pups we had no problems with any of the other animals, though Fluffy, true to form, kept a watchful eye on their upbringing, and we can certainly thank him for the speed with which the puppies became house-trained.

I was a bit concerned when my wife brought home a baby guineapig. When it arrived it was no bigger than a mouse, and I was afraid that Fluffy might lay violent claws on the little creature. But I could have spared myself this anxiety. Fluffy poked at it for a bit with one forepaw, rolled it over on its back and inspected it with painstaking curiosity. Then he gave a nod of approval, and that was that.

Even if it had been a mouse, the same thing would undoubtedly have happened. The little creature belonged to the house, and that was all that was needed for Fluffy and the other animals. We saw the clearest examples of this at a later date when we started feeding a host of birds on the veranda. Some of these birds, notably a pair of titmice, grew so tame that they came in through the open veranda door whenever they pleased. One of them got into the habit of perching on Bamse's head for a rest, while the other used to spend the night in the living-room, where it sat and slept on top of a cupboard that was Fluffy's favourite place during the day. None of the animals touched these birds—because they belonged to the house. Fluffy, on the other hand, would sneak over to our neighbour's yard and catch birds of the same species when he wanted a change of menu.

Not only did Fluffy leave the birds on the veranda in peace; he even made sure that *we* treated them properly. The birds used to come for their breakfast as soon as it began to grow light, and during the summer this could be distinctly early. If we didn't wake up in time to put out the food, there would be a regular uproar outside. If that didn't wake us, Fluffy would repair the omission by sitting on our pillow and slapping our faces with his paw. We soon learned to use our wits and put out the food the night before if we wanted to sleep in peace in the morning.

It is beyond question that animals of all species can live together in peace and toleration. There is no hatred or fear in animals in the sense in which we experience these feelings, and the only thing needed to get animals to live together in peace is to show them the way and set them a good example. Our own animals have always had the sense of *belonging*: they were always members of a big family, all of whom received the same respect and affection. In time, our animals adopted the same outlook as we had ourselves—and every creature that was accepted by us was automatically accepted by the animals.

All of them—lion, cat, dog, rabbit, skunk, guineapig, birds—lived with us without friction. All of them learned that we have to stick together in order to find happiness in life, and that the sick and weak must be protected. The best proof of this was the occasion when Bamse came and led me out into the forest where he had found a half-dead Siamese cat, who had been brutally hit and sent flying by a car, and had then crept away from the road and tried to crawl under an old hut to lie down and die in peace.

We took the cat home, brought him back to life by all the resources of modern medical science—including an oxygen mask—and for the three weeks that this lasted Bamse never left the 'sickbed' except to eat or obey a call of nature. Fluffy, who as a rule could not endure other cats, displayed equal concern for the invalid, because we had taken it into the house.

It is when one attains this interdependence that it becomes a real joy to have animals around, a joy that we have been privileged to experience in the highest degree.

Everybody can achieve the same contact with their animals as we did with ours. All animals, wild or tame, will try to give pleasure and satisfaction to the human beings they like and trust. A child can usually do anything it likes with an animal, because the animal understands the child's uncomplicated, innocent nature. There are no destructive forces at work in the child's mind—that is something that comes later—and so animals trust him.

The adult human being can achieve the same as the child, even if it takes a bit more effort. Simple child psychology will usually open many doors. In addition, it is necessary to show the animal that you are fond of him, that you have sympathy, understanding and respect for him. But this respect must be mutual. If you shower an animal with too much affection, this respect is lost and the relationship destroyed. The animal must feel that it can turn to man for help and protection, and it must then meet with strength and resolution. If these are lacking it is a sign of weakness, and a weak person is not to be trusted in times of need.

SEVENTEEN

CLARENCE
THE CROSS-EYED LION

During my extensive travels I have often found myself face to face with 'the king of beasts', but I had never been on talking terms with him before I met Clarence, the famous cross-eyed lion who played the lead role in the 'Daktari' series, as well as in several independent feature films.

Clarence was basically just as untamed as any lion roaming the wilds of his African homeland. Although he was quite young when captured, he had been born free and raised by his parents in the true traditions of the great cats. In 'Africa, USA' he was never subjected to any of the old-fashioned training methods which consist of intimidating and beating an animal into terror-stricken submission to his human tormentor.

There were no whips in 'Africa, USA'. Any physical or mental brutality—even raising the voice in anger—was strictly forbidden. The only method used in the compound was the so-called 'affection training' devised by the joint owners, Ralph Helfer and Ivan Tors. This method is based on the theory that if an animal is given respect, understanding and love, he will respond in kind. Those who are acquainted with 'Africa, USA' and 'Daktari' know that the method is unbelievably effective.

This was the only training Clarence ever had, and his pride, his dignity and his feeling of personal freedom remained intact throughout his life. He was treated by the handlers and the actors with the respect due to the king of animals, and his respect for his human friends was equally high. He insisted on being addressed in a polite and friendly manner, and in return he offered total loyalty. He seemed to realize that humans had many weaknesses which he didn't have. For reasons of safety his claws had been pulled, but his giant fangs were fully intact and he was just as capable of defending himself as ever. The removal of his claws had not been due to mistrust; he could have killed a human being with a single swipe of his tremendous paw if such a thought had ever entered his mind. The reason was simply that Ivan Tors wanted to prevent the repetition of an incident he had witnessed in Kenya, when a woman was accidentally killed while playing with a lion. During the game the woman fell and the lion put his paw on her neck. In his excitement he forgot to keep his big, razor-sharp claws 'sheathed', with the result that when the woman tried to roll away from him she got her throat ripped out.

In 1963 Clarence, together with a half dozen other lion cubs, arrived in 'Africa, USA' direct from the wilds of Kenya. The actor Marshall Thompson was there when they arrived. His attention was immediately attracted by a chubby little fellow, bow-legged and unbelievably cross-eyed. He dubbed him 'Clarence'—for no other reason than that it seemed a fitting name. As the cub also soon revealed himself a born comedian he was referred to equally often as the 'clown-prince' of 'Africa, USA'.

He was barely two years old when he rose to fame through his role in Ivan Tors' two comedy films *Clarence—The Cross-Eyed Lion* and *Clarence Returns*. But it was through his role in the 'Daktari' series that his name—and his face—became known to millions of people round the world. Like Ben Turpin, Clarence had his squint to thank for his rapid rise to world fame. His comic talents and magnetic personality would have brought him to stardom in any event, but it would have taken longer. No wonder he was valued by his owners at a million dollars.

When I was first introduced to Clarence I must admit that I felt rather small. But after he had licked my hand as a sign of acceptance, we became the best of friends. During the next two years I spent a great deal of time with him, and the better I got to know him the more I respected and admired him.

On the film set he was most co-operative, and nobody needed to order him around. If anyone tried, Clarence would look at him disdainfully, yawn, turn his back to the camera and walk away. If asked politely, however, he would joyfully do anything. It was not that he particularly liked all

the strange things his human friends wanted him to do, but he felt it gave them pleasure. And he liked to please his friends who were so kind, and fed him so well.

Clarence when full-grown was a truly magnificent specimen. With his five hundred pounds of concentrated bone and muscle he was a giant even among male lions. He was also uncommonly good-natured and nothing seemed to ruffle him. His best friend, Judy the chimpanzee, could be a real pest in her most mischievous moments, and Clarence suffered many indignities from her. But he never succumbed to his natural instincts, which would have been to remove his tormentor once and for all with a swipe of his paw or a snap of his jaws. When she became too much to endure, he would simply get to his feet and walk majestically away to find a spot where he would be left in peace.

Clarence was as lazy as he was good-natured, which caused the directors no end of frustration. To them time was expensive, while it meant nothing to Clarence. He placidly participated in the play-acting until he tired of it. Then he would calmly walk off-stage in the middle of a 'take'. No power under the sun could bring him back on the job until he was in the mood. In fact, as an actor, he belonged to the 'mood school', as the professionals call it. That is, he would only act when he felt like it. Paul Landres, who directed more than half the 'Daktari' episodes, said that very little was needed to distract him from his work. A leaf fluttering on the wind, a beam of sunlight playing on a piece of glass or metal, the least movement of any kind, was enough to catch his interest. Nothing could then entice him back to work until his curiosity had been entirely satisfied.

Poor Clarence was more cross-eyed than any other creature I have ever seen. During the first weeks, Ralph Helfer and Ivan Tors paid little attention to this. According to experts a great many lion cubs are born cross-eyed, but their eyes generally straighten out during early youth. But as the months passed by without any visible improvements, the owners started to worry. Ivan Tors, whom *Life Magazine* at one time dubbed 'the most loving animal lover in the world', decided that no money must be spared to help get

Clarence's sight straightened out. The regular veterinarian of the compound could do nothing, and so Clarence was taken to the leading eye specialist in the State of California —a professor at the Medical School of the University in Los Angeles. After lengthy examinations the learned professor concluded that nothing would be gained by surgery, but that the eyes could possibly be straightened by means of corrective glasses.

Clarence was fitted with a pair of expensive spectacles and for a long time everyone did their best to make him wear them. But he was equally determined not to. He put up a bitter fight and whenever the handlers got the spectacles attached to his head, he tore them off again. The outcome of this uneven battle was that Clarence emerged the victor, and the attempt to straighten his eyes was abandoned.

In the compound, of course, it didn't matter whether he had double vision or not, but in his own environment he would not have survived very long. Everything he looked at would appear double. A hunted antelope would look like two and whichever one he leaped at he would miss, since the animal itself would be located somewhere in between. Had Clarence been forced to hunt for his food he would soon have starved to death, but fortunately for him he did not have to worry about the next meal. Anyone who ever knew Clarence intimately will agree that he was quite content with his double vision and that it didn't bother him in the least in his daily life. During his first three years at 'Africa, USA' he discovered that if he really wanted to see straight he could do it simply by closing one eye, and looking through the other.

Clarence was perfectly happy as long as his human friends showered him with affection and fed him his twelve pounds of good fresh meat per day. These were the only things he demanded from life, and I must admit that I often envied him his uncomplicated philosophy.

Maybe it was this philosophy that made Clarence so lazy. All he had to do for his keep was to participate in a bit of play-acting from time to time. He was fed and cared for, so why should he exert himself? Consequently, he refused to do anything which might put a strain upon him, such as running. Whenever such actions were needed for a scene, a stand-in had to be provided. And Clarence is, to my knowledge, the only animal film star who had a permanently employed stand-in for his more strenuous roles.

He could exert himself when he wanted to, however, and I have seen Clarence in action on several occasions. Many animal scenes were shot in 'Africa, USA' at the request of other film makers, and on one occasion a strange demand was received from a director in New York. This man was making a film, set in Africa, in which an Alsatian dog saved his master's life by engaging an attacking lion in battle and driving him off. Could Helfer provide this scene?

Helfer accepted the order, well aware that he might have some problems. The only lion in the compound who could be trusted in a scene of this nature was Clarence, and the only dog he could possibly use was his own big Alsatian, Prince. Helfer was sure that Clarence would never hurt Prince, since the two were the best of friends, but the big problem would be to get Prince to attack Clarence in a realistic manner.

First of all Prince had to be toughened up. To achieve this he was banished from the compound and turned loose in the barren hinterlands surrounding 'Africa, USA'. There he had to fend for himself for a full week, hunting for his food and getting lean, strong and supple. When he got back to the compound he was in perfect shape, hungry and slightly short-tempered. And then followed the brief, but hectic, drilling of the two opponents.

I was present when the actual battle took place in front of the camera, and it was one of the most violent fights I have ever witnessed. The two combatants went for each other with a convincing show of fury; and I am sure even Ralph Helfer suffered some anxious moments while the fight lasted, because it looked as if the two really had murder in their hearts. Time and again Clarence aimed mighty swipes at the dog with his huge paws, and each time Prince cleverly evaded the dangerous blows. Equally often Prince would dive in and sink his fangs in Clarence's throat —though in reality he was careful only to grab hold of his thick heavy mane. On several occasions it looked as if

Clarence would succeed in getting Prince's head between his powerful jaws and crush it, but Prince managed every time to dodge him at the very last moment.

The scene ended when the lion, with defiant roars, pulled back into the underbrush and disappeared in the jungle—defeated by the heroic dog! With all due respect to Alsatians, this was a highly improbable ending, but that was how the director wanted it.

It had been a bloodless fight with the exception of a small scratch on one of Prince's ears, inflicted by the snapping fangs of the great lion when he had slightly misjudged the distance. Clarence seemed heartbroken over this misfortune and kept licking his friend's ear until the doctor arrived and dabbed iodine on the scratch.

On another occasion Clarence was playing the role of a lion killed by a poacher in a protected area. For a brief moment he had to remain completely motionless while the close-up of the 'dead' lion was being filmed. But on that particular day Clarence was not in his most co-operative mood, and time and again the scene had to be cut because of his bungling. Either he blinked at the crucial moment, or he sighed deeply—causing his flanks to heave—or he whisked his tail to chase off a fly. In short, he did everything a dead lion would not do.

Finally Helfer lost his patience and ordered Clarence off-stage, and then he was given the ultimate punishment—the cold shoulder. Clarence, so badly in need of his daily measure of affection, tried to endear himself to every handler and actor in turn. The result was always the same, everyone turned his back on him and pretended he didn't exist. In the end Clarence broke down. He searched out Ralph Helfer, laid himself down at his feet and begged forgiveness with his big, yellow, crossed eyes.

Ralph felt that Clarence had probably been punished enough. In a grave voice he admonished him for his behaviour and ordered him back on the set. And this time the scene went without a hitch. Clarence couldn't have played his role better if he had really been dead. Long after the order 'Cut!' was sounded he remained motionless, holding his breath. He wasn't going to make another mistake and endure such cruel punishment again.

Like human beings, and all other warm-blooded animals, Clarence could be bad-tempered sometimes, and then it was advisable to keep at a distance. . . . It might be a headache or an upset stomach that bothered him. He would warn everyone with a special roar that told them clearly to stay away. All his fellow actors in 'Africa, USA' had studied his moods and accepted his warning without question. Even Judy would keep at a safe distance when Clarence indicated that he wouldn't tolerate disturbance of any kind.

Every so often Clarence would amble over to the fenced area where the antelopes were grazing. Once I watched him licking a new-born antelope calf who under ordinary circumstances would have made an excellent lunch snack. But Clarence was fed regularly and was never hungry—and a lion kills only when he needs food.

He used to visit the animal nursery regularly to play with the youngsters of various species. He seemed to enjoy playing with wolf- and dog-whelps, lambs and calves, just as much as with the cubs of leopards, tigers and lions. He was a paragon of patience and extremely careful not to harm or scare the little creatures. They, on the other hand, seemed to have no fear of him and could be quite rough when they attacked him *en masse* and sank their sharp little teeth and claws into his tail and legs.

Clarence was one of the few animals in 'Africa, USA' who never had to be locked up. He had his own cage, like all the other animals, but the door was left open, allowing him to come and go as he pleased. If he wanted to be undisturbed he would retire to the sleeping quarters, and he knew that nobody would bother him there.

On occasions, when Helfer wanted him to stay put in a specific place, Clarence was tied to a pole in the ground. He could have torn himself loose with the greatest ease, but this never occurred to him. His friends wanted him to stay put, and that was a wish he always respected.

In July 1969, Clarence died very suddenly while on a guest performance in Florida. Neither his regular handlers nor his veterinarian were along on the trip, or he might have survived. It was a common, innocent kitten illness which struck him in the prime of life. This virus, while quite harmless to young kittens, can be dangerous to grown animals unless treated properly and quickly.

Clarence probably got ill during the night, but although the handler realized that he was not well in the morning when he attended to him he thought nothing more of it. During the afternoon it became evident that Clarence was very sick and a vet was called. An antibiotics injection could probably still have saved him, and he was given a shot—but within the hour he was dead. The measure of antibiotics had been either too weak or too strong.

The death of Clarence was a painful loss to all who knew him, and effectively barred any thoughts of continuing the 'Daktari' series.

EIGHTEEN   JUDY THE CHIMPANZEE

'Another lump of sugar, Judy?' I asked the young creature opposite me. We were having a last cup of coffee together before I left California. Judy nodded and grinned gratefully, at the same time indicating that she wouldn't mind a puff or two of my cigarette. I glanced around guardedly before giving it to her—it wouldn't do to be caught leading her astray. Quickly, and with obvious relish, she puffed deeply two or three times, and then returned it to me.

Judy was not allowed to smoke, although she liked it so much. It might be habit-forming, and there are certain vices an aspiring actress should not succumb to. But she was given a puff once in a while, and really enjoyed it. She never inhaled the smoke. She just kept it in her mouth, and let it sift out slowly through her nose and pouted lips. I have seen her making perfect smoke rings.

As a rule, Judy behaved perfectly, although once in a while she forgot herself—as all teenagers do—and acted in an unladylike fashion. But girls will be girls, and it is easy to forgive them when they are as enchanting as Judy; particularly since Judy is not an ordinary teenager, but a chimpanzee.

She loved coffee, and whenever I visited the compound of 'Africa, USA', to watch them shoot another 'Daktari' episode, I had a cup of coffee with her during one of the breaks. The ritual was always the same. I would fill our cup from the big container and bring them to the table. I would then offer her cream and sugar; she would help herself and pass it on to me. She would stir her coffee gracefully with a spoon and then sip it like a true lady, holding the cup daintily by the handle. Her manners would hardly have been conspicuous even in the best of Hollywood restaurants.

Judy needs no introduction to those who have had the good fortune to watch 'Daktari' on television. The series was filmed for six years in the USA and has been shown in

138

some sixty countries round the world. A new episode was filmed every week, and although Marshall Thompson had the lead billing as the 'Daktari' of the show, there is no question who the real star was—Judy.

Judy could not, of course, read her own lines—but then she didn't have a speaking part. She plainly longed to talk, and was forever trying, but the tongue of the chimpanzee is incapable of forming words. To make up for it, however, she tried to make herself understood by sign language; and it has proved beyond any doubt that she understood more than two hundred commonly used words and expressions.

Judy could cry, smile and laugh. But facial expression alone would not have got her very far had she not also been able to act. And it was here that Judy excelled.

When Judy appears before the film camera she becomes a thoroughly polished actor. While she is waiting around the set for her scene to be shot she enjoys herself in her own playful way. But the moment the 'on camera' signal sounds she becomes a complete professional. She listens intently to her orders, and carries them out with suave perfection. During my many visits to the set I never knew Judy to misunderstand an instruction—which would frequently have taxed the average human ability.

I was extremely impressed by Judy's performance in a scene in one episode. She was in the back of a truck, hidden under a sheet of canvas which was tied down at all four corners. She reached her hand out from under the canvas and untied the line which fastened one corner. Then she jumped down, looked carefully round and ran up to the cab of the truck. She climbed into the driver's seat, removed the key from the ignition and flung it among the bushes. Having done this she returned to the back of the truck and, looking around once more to make sure she had not been observed, climbed back on to the truck and tied down the canvas exactly as it had been before.

The entire scene was filmed in one 'take'—after she had been shown the sequence only once before shooting started—and she made no mistakes. It takes a brain of almost human capacity to remember all these details.

In another scene Judy had 'adopted' a small black panther

kitten. The script required that she should take him out of the compound, and before the filming she had been shown what to do. She tied a length of packing-twine around his neck and walked into the jungle with him 'on leash'. She did this as easily as if she did it every day. But then the panther kitten suddenly started to struggle against the string. Judy did exactly as she had been shown to do earlier, if such an emergency should arise: she lifted the little kitten up in her arms, cuddled it against her chest and caressed it until it relaxed. Then she put it down again and they continued on their way into the bush. No mother could have played that part more convincingly than Judy.

This was excellent acting, but it was also a quite natural thing for her to do. Although very young, she had a highly developed mother-instinct. She loved young animals dearly, and more than once she had been caught sneaking into the compound 'infirmary' to steal a little cub, whether it was lion, tiger or her 'natural enemy', the leopard.

Her love for the other animals in the compound had become one of Ralph Helfer's great problems. All animals in 'Africa, USA' were untamed in the conventional way, although they had learned to live with each other and with humans. But there were a number of leopards and jaguars walking around, with only a chain around their necks, and these animals were by nature the greatest threat to monkeys. In the beginning Judy had the ape's instinctive fear of them, but that fear eventually disappeared and she took so many liberties with them that everyone thought it would end in disaster. The leopard mother might well forget herself if she caught Judy trying to steal her cub.

If Clarence, the Cross-Eyed Lion, was the king of 'Africa, USA', then Judy without question was the Queen. She skipped around in the compound, among more than five hundred animals, and chattered to everyone in sight—human or animal. But she was also, like all ladies—and particularly film stars—unpredictable and apt to throw tantrums. She could be very jealous of any other animal who took the limelight in a show. In her own opinion she was the one and only star and she insisted on being treated accordingly. If she got the impression that another animal was being favoured, she might act up just as badly as an Elizabeth Taylor or a Maria Callas. Force would not compel her to behave in a proper manner—psychology must be applied.

An example of this, which I shall never forget, happened during the filming of an episode in which two bank robbers had buried their loot inside the Wameru compound. Judy, hidden among the bushes, followed their every move. Later she dug up the money box and hid it somewhere else. A convent nearby had run out of money and would have to shut down unless the nuns could get financial assistance. They approached 'Daktari' Tracy for help, but as he also was out of available funds the case seemed hopeless—until Judy brought the loot to the prioress.

Towards the end of the episode the prioress comes to the Wameru compound—Daktari's study centre—to thank Judy for her help. According to the script she lifts Judy up in her arms and hugs her. Judy is then supposed to give her a resounding kiss on the cheek. The scene had to be re-taken ten times while I was watching, because it always ended the same way. At the crucial moment—instead of kissing the prioress—Judy would turn her head in utter disgust. She was upset because earlier in the episode the cast had paid a great deal of attention to a small lion cub who also had a part in the show.

The part of the prioress was played by Ann Bancroft, and it must have been rather unusual for her to have someone refuse to kiss her. But Ralph Helfer finally settled the matter. He took Judy aside and spoke seriously to her. 'Listen, Judy, if you don't cut it out and get the kissing done with, there will be no coffee afterwards!' That did it. She decided to swallow her pride. The next play of the scene went perfectly, and I have seldom seen Judy kiss anybody so heartily in all the time I have known her. When the satisfied director shouted 'Cut!', she turned her back disdainfully on Ann Bancroft and scampered over to the coffee-table to collect her promised reward.

Judy's most notable characteristics are refinement, courage, inquisitiveness and a warm heart. She is also endowed with great beauty; compare her with any other chimpanzee, and you will agree. She is nearly always good tempered, despite the fact that, like all famous actors, she leads a very hectic life. Daily shootings of 'Daktari' episodes, interviews, modelling and personal appearances outside the compound are only a part of her daily life.

She is a first rate P.R. ape, and seems to understand the importance of the press. When she hears a camera click, she knows that a picture has been taken, and reacts instantly by taking up another position, or moving over to some other background.

Pens and pencils fascinate her. She knows which end to use, and often during an interview will grab the pen and block from a visiting reporter to show that she, too, knows the art of writing. She will fill a page or two with scribble—then proudly show what she has 'written' to everyone around, before giving the pen and block back to their rightful owner.

Opinions about Judy's level of intelligence vary greatly. Ivan Tors is conservative in his estimate and claims that Judy has an intelligence equal to that of a child of six; her handlers say that she can match any ten-year-old child, while her human co-stars in the 'Daktari' show agreed that she is simply a genius. Be that as it may—one thing is certain: Judy is a happy and friendly creature who has done well in show-business and who, thanks to the tremendous impact of TV, is loved by more people all over the world than any other chimpanzee in history—including the famous Cheeta from the old Tarzan films.

Judy loved Clarence, and Clarence in turn was undoubtedly very fond of her. He let her play pranks on him that he would not tolerate from anyone else. Whenever she could, she got tit-bits for him from the animal kitchen—particularly really juicy bones. But Clarence also liked sweet things, like whipped cream, in small portions. I once saw Judy with a bowlful which she had been permitted to bring her friend. She scooped up a handful and stuffed it in his mouth. Clarence accepted it, but then he was satisfied and refused a second helping. This did not suit Judy. The bowl of cream was for Clarence, and he was going to have it, one way or another. She forgot her manners completely;

positioned herself directly in front of him and started tossing handful after handful into his face, until his entire head was covered by the sticky stuff. He growled a warning at her once or twice, but then gave it up as hopeless, got to his feet and strode majestically away—with Judy hanging on to his tail.

Of all those who mourned Clarence's death nobody felt the loss stronger than Judy. When she finally realized that her friend Clarence was gone for good it was a shock almost too much to bear. She lost her spirit, could no longer find pleasure in acting, and for a long time refused to eat. She was given a long vacation, and although she overcame the worst of her grief, she lost the spark that had brought her to stardom.

Judy was born in Africa and raised and reared free, but she was not very old before she was trapped and sent to America. There she was purchased by an elderly couple who wanted her for a pet. But it soon turned out that Judy was anything but that; on the contrary she was a problem child of the worst kind, a regular juvenile delinquent. Before long she had taken over the entire house and was terrorizing her adoptive parents. If anything was denied her, she would grow completely wild; she would scream and bite, and throw everything around that she could lay her hands on.

Finally, in desperation, the elderly couple telephoned Ralph Helfer and begged him to take her off their hands. 'Please get her out of here before she tears the house down', they implored him. Ralph drove by the same day and picked her up. And that's how Judy came to 'Africa, USA'.

Weeks passed by, but the problem child refused to respond to Helfer's 'affection training', despite the fact that this method—which turns lions and tigers into lambs—had never failed before. One of the handlers, who had been assigned to Judy, told me that she always carried a little rag doll which her first owners had given her. She wouldn't allow anybody to touch this doll, let alone take it away from her. In due course she bit three handlers who attempted to.

But the affection lavished on her by the combined staff of 'Africa, USA' finally began to tell. The first sign was when Judy condescended to accept a banana from her handler.

Then she let herself be patted on the head. And one day—to everybody's great surprise—she jumped into his arms and gave him a hearty hug. But for a long time after this she continued to carry her rag doll with her wherever she went. It was only when she began to accept the challenge of learning that she finally discarded the doll. It may sound like something from a psychiatrist's case-book, and in fact Judy's case was not very different from that of a human child. Love, confidence and respect—challenge and reward—that is the only treatment needed.

Judy, as all her friends agree, is not just an ordinary animal. They treat her and talk to her like a fellow human being. Once when another chimpanzee had torn off one of her finger nails, I remember her gratitude when I blew on the sore finger. I remember the many chilly autumn days, with the cold wind sweeping down from the mountains, when Judy would sit shivering between 'takes'. On many occasions she would gratefully borrow my warm windbreaker, which she put on just the way I did myself, with the zipper pulled up as far as it would go. She appreciated that small attention very much, and I think we became true friends during that period.

I like to believe that she understood me when I told her that I had to leave and that I would be gone for a long time. As she gave me a last hug, she was desperately trying to tell me something—but she only managed the usual 'oh, oh, oh' sounds. But I think I got her message anyway, and I like to believe that what she said was: 'Don't forget us while you are gone—and remember that we will welcome you back!'

NINETEEN

From my study I could hear the patter of a dog's paws in the hallway outside. The door was pushed open and the dog sat down next to me at the desk. Engrossed in my work I didn't even look up. 'Hello, junior, how's my boy today?' I asked, as I stretched out my hand and patted his head, still not looking up.

Normally, in the early morning hours, Tor would be with Ciska, 'helping' her with the housework. But she had just left to see a neighbour who had called and asked for her advice on some matter. So Tor had come in to stay with me, lying quietly at my feet while I worked.

Suddenly I felt his paw on my thigh, scratching urgently, and I looked at him to see what he wanted. He was sitting down, looking at me expectantly, and between his teeth he gingerly held Ciska's 'Miss Dior' *eau de cologne* bottle.

The touch of irritation I had felt at being disturbed vanished. It was not the first time he had done this, and I found the situation as comical every time. I also knew what was required of me. 'Really, Tor, you could have waited till Ciska came back, you know', I told him as I took the bottle from his jaws. I opened it, moistened my fingertip and gave him a dab of perfume behind each ear. Wagging his tail happily Tor grabbed the bottle out of my hand, raced back to the bedroom and put it carefully on Ciska's dressing table, in the exact spot where he had found it.

This was part of the daily morning ritual between Ciska and Tor. He had to be combed and brushed; then as Ciska went over the carpets with the vacuum cleaner he would jump on to the bed, where Ciska had spread his personal sheet, to have his coat vacuumed. He would patiently stand by while Ciska did her morning toilet at the dressing table, waiting for the final touch to his own, gentleman's grooming. He would stand behind her on his hind legs, front paws on the back of her chair, head over her right shoulder, watching every detail in the mirror with fascination, and growing more excited until the ultimate moment when Ciska uncorked the cologne bottle—then he would get his dab and the day would be ready to begin, and only then.

Tor was a big dog, almost a year old, but he had been with us virtually since birth. I remember vividly how we got him.

We were living in California, high up in the Sierra Nevada mountains. Because of my extensive travelling we had no animals with us, and my wife sorely missed a companion. One day she saw an ad in the local newspaper, 'Home sought for two puppies', and I immediately called the number to make an appointment.

The big rambling framehouse in the huge garden just outside town was occupied by an old couple in their late seventies, and eighteen dogs of all breeds and mixes. They had recently had two litters of puppies and, much to their regret, had had to dispose of some of them. Unfortunately, the two they wanted to give away were small dogs, typical lap-dogs, and that was not what we had in mind.

The other bitch with a litter was an Australian sheep dog. They are known to be very intelligent animals and were just the right size for us. Apart from being fine working dogs, they also make good companions and excellent protectors. The bitch was lying on the floor, her two puppies between her front paws. One of them was like the mother with a curly, tan coat. The other was dark, almost black, with some white on his chest. And he was the one who caught our attention.

There was something strangely familiar about him as he lay spreadeagled on the floor, his short, stubby legs stretched out in four different directions. But I could not think what it was until Ciska whispered: 'Isn't he just the picture of Bamse at that age?' And that was it—a fat little fellow with small, clever eyes and a thick, heavy coat that seemed to be a half dozen sizes too big for him.

We fell for him immediately, which he seemed to sense, because he got to his feet with some difficulty and ambled over to Ciska. He then did a sort of dance until Ciska picked

him up, and a bond was struck which I knew could never be severed.

But he was only four weeks old and too young to be taken from his mother. The old people promised not to give him to anybody else and suggested we pick him up in about two weeks. As it happened, however, it was my birthday eight days later, and we travelled out to visit the old people and take another look at 'our dog' on that day.

He was full of life and spirits now and made for Ciska the moment we stepped inside. When I took a walk around the property a little later he followed me like a shadow, always 'at heel', stumbling along on his short, bowed legs. Once inside again he took possession of Ciska. It was obvious that he had adopted us, rather than the other way round, and he was making sure that we didn't slip out of his grasp as we had done the first time. The old couple decided he had better go with us that day, in spite of his tender age.

We hadn't quite made up our mind what to call him, but after the first night in our home his name came to me quite naturally. It had to be 'Tor', from old Nordic mythology— the war god who governed thunder and lightning. He was all over the house like a thunderstorm, fighting with shoes and other loose objects, barking at Ciska till she lifted him up on her bed and then attacking her toes and fingers with his small, needle-sharp teeth, until he slipped off the bed again. And then it was my turn.

He soon discovered, however, that I was not quite so much fun as Ciska. I would try to ignore him, pull the blanket over my head and roll away from him. At times I would kick with my legs, which he didn't like at all. So he would lie flat on his belly on my bed, watching Ciska intently. She couldn't help sneaking a look at him with one eye, and immediately he would be off my bed in a flash for another merry-go-round with Ciska.

By four in the morning we were all exhausted, and Tor was put lovingly, but firmly, to bed in his own little box in the kitchen, where he slept soundly till almost noon that day.

Only a day or two elapsed before he started to tell us when he needed to go out, and we never had any problem with house-training. The second day in our home he even told Ciska, in his own manner, that their morning walk in the woods was overdue. We were sitting in the kitchen over a cup of coffee when Tor suddenly disappeared into the bedroom, where he made quite a racket. Thinking that he was playing, we paid no attention until suddenly he appeared in the kitchen, dragging one of Ciska's heavy walking shoes along with him. He had a hard struggle, since the shoe was as big and heavy as he was, but he managed to haul it over to Ciska's chair where he dropped it. Then he made a dash for the bedroom to fetch the other shoe, and sat down expectantly in front of Ciska. He was a very proud dog when she got the message and took him for a walk.

Tor as a puppy was so ugly that only his mother could have found him attractive, but his intelligence was outstanding. I don't think I have ever known a more intelligent dog. And his puppy ugliness was deceptive, because as he grew up he became more beautiful by the month. His thick heavy coat became progressively lighter and he ended up a light silky brown on the back and a golden tan on the flanks. He had a broad forehead, brown clever eyes and long, hanging ears with a mass of golden curls. He used to flip up one ear, covering the top of his head like a mini-beret.

Early in September, quite unexpectedly, I had to take a trip to Canada and then to Europe. Ciska had to come with me, and we planned to take Tor along to the ranch in Canada. But then we found out that he could not cross the border without the regulation shots, and the vet refused to give these before he was three months old. Tor would only be ten weeks by that time, so we were forced to board him in his old home until we got back. He was so unhappy that he had to be tied up when we prepared to drive away.

The trip, supposed to be five weeks, dragged out and it was seven weeks before we returned. As we drove up towards the gate of the old house, we noticed a dog sitting on a chair on the glass-enclosed veranda. I didn't recognize him at first glance, but Ciska did. At the same moment as she called out 'There's Tor!' I saw the dog lift his head and look towards us with disbelief all over his face. He had recognized the sound of the car, but couldn't believe his ears. The veranda door was closed, but one of the window panes had been broken and was temporarily covered by a piece of cardboard. Tor dived straight through it, taking with him pieces of glass and window frame, and made straight for the car.

Ciska had opened the door to step out, but she never had a chance. Tor shot in through the half-opened door like a flash and jumped in our laps, whimpering with happiness. He refused to leave the car again and stayed in it until we were ready to drive home with him.

We learned that he had been sitting on the veranda every hour of the day since our departure, watching all cars going by and listening for the special sound of ours. The only time he would leave his look-out was when he played with the other dogs; he never strayed far from the front gate, and cut his meals in the kitchen as short as possible.

It was indeed a changed dog that we got back. He had grown tremendously, and his coat had turned very light. The old man had put a thong of leather around his neck, which had worn away the hair. He had been well fed, but he hadn't been groomed since we left him and he looked a mess. His heavy coat was caked with filth, and we decided that his first stop in our new home would be the bath tub. The old people had done their best for him, but by this time they had twenty-four dogs and they just couldn't manage to care for Tor in the way he was used to.

I carried him into the house like a bride, and while I ran a tub-full of hot water Ciska made Tor acquainted with every room in the house, and put a bed of blankets in front of the fireplace. Since he had never had a bath before I expected Tor to put up quite a struggle when I lifted him and plunged him into the steaming water. But to our great surprise he enjoyed the new experience immensely. While he was being shampooed and scrubbed he splashed about in the tub, having a wonderful time. If possible, he enjoyed the towelling and grooming afterwards even more.

During the months following, Tor had many baths, for he had a tremendous ability to get himself dirty. If there happened to be a pool of stagnant, slimy water within a mile of the house, Tor would blunder into it somehow. I began to suspect that he did it on purpose to get a hot bath. If we missed him during the daytime, and knew he was indoors, we only had to check in the bathroom, where he would invariably be, taking a nap in the tub.

Our neighbours had a big black Labrador named Spade. He and Tor became great friends and although Spade was only half a year older than Tor he seemed to regard him as a kid brother whom he had to guide and protect. Tor's life would have been much more difficult without Spade, because there were a lot of stray dogs around who would try to pick a fight with the puppy. But Spade always turned up at the crucial moment and intervened.

After our first 'disappearance' Tor never got over his fear of losing us. He was most unhappy if he came home and found one of us gone. If we were both gone he would become completely frantic, as we once witnessed from a neighbour's window. After that we made sure that he was never left alone again.

Like all puppies Tor was extremely playful, but he preferred games that taxed his ability and intelligence. One of his favourite games was hide-and-seek. And I can't remember a single time that he failed to retrieve a hidden object, wherever we put it. On one occasion I hid his rubber ball in an empty tin can with a lid on. I placed the can among several similar cans on a shelf above the kitchen sink, and then went back to the living-room and told Tor to find his ball.

His superior sense of smell soon brought him out into the kitchen, but there he seemed to be momentarily lost. But his confusion lasted only a minute or so. Suddenly he jumped up and put his front paws on the kitchen sink, his nose pointing to the tin cans high above him and his tail wagging enthusiastically.

I grabbed one of the empty tin cans and showed it to him, but he only gave me an impatient glance, then focused his attention on the shelf again. Asking 'Is it here?' I put my hand in quick succession on one tin after the other. The moment my hand touched the tin containing the ball, he barked. I did it all over again, but he only barked when I touched the right tin.

Above all he loved to play hide-and-seek with Ciska. He would put on a great act, searching everywhere until finally he got to her—having known all the time exactly where she was hiding.

With me he invented a game of football. He would bring his ball to me at one end of our long living-room. Then he would run to the opposite wall and take up position between two chairs. I was supposed to be the centre-forward and he the goal-keeper. I must shamefacedly admit that I rarely scored a goal against him.

Immediately after returning from our long trip we had bought Tor a beautiful collar and fitted on it the two metal tags for registration and inoculation. He had obviously seen other dogs wearing them, and had probably felt rather undressed without one. Consequently he was extremely proud of his new collar and refused to go outside without it.

His love and loyalty were boundless, and when one day he refused to get in the car with us I became worried. Normally, he was first in the car, but today he was so reluctant to get in that I almost had to force him. He was promptly ill. The next day he flatly refused to go along for a drive. Having had similar experiences before with a dog, I decided to have the car checked, and this precaution possibly saved our lives.

It turned out that Tor knew more about automobiles than I did. It was discovered that there was a hole in the exhaust pipe, which was letting poisonous fumes into the car. I hadn't noticed, but it had made Tor sick. And worse, the steel bar connecting the steering column with the driving wheels had developed a crack and was in danger of separating completely at any moment. This break had created a vibration and an unfamiliar sound which to Tor's sensitive ear spelt danger. Driving down the steep mountain road on our next trip to town would probably have caused the final parting of the bar—and death and destruction for us. My admiration for Tor rose by several degrees as a result.

After the car had been repaired, Tor had no more worries about driving. On the contrary, it was as though he began to take an interest in what made the automobile tick. He found out, possibly by watching me, how to sound the horn, and he used his new-found knowledge whenever he felt it was appropriate. He hated being left in the car when we went shopping, and after we had been in the store about five minutes he would start signalling us with blasts at regular intervals until we turned up. In the end, if his signalling didn't produce results, he went even further. He would simply turn round and sit down on the button, producing one long, continuous and nerve-shattering blast.

As he grew up it became abundantly clear that, as we had thought from the very first moment, Tor was no more than 50 per cent Australian sheep dog. Who his father was we never found out, but we suspected a big golden retriever a frequent guest in the area of the old couple's house. Tor's mother, who was of a rather frivolous nature, seemed to have a special affection for that particular dog. Whoever the father was, the mixture produced one of the most outstanding dogs I have ever had the good fortune to meet.

TWENTY   A FEW WORDS ON ANIMAL PSYCHOLOGY

To understand animals—wild or tame—you must first try to understand their mentality. They have different criteria of what is right and wrong, what is natural and un-natural—in short, what one can and cannot do. In these matters an animal's thought-processes are primitive—on a level with those of early man. His actions are dictated by instinct.

When two dogs copulate in the street they are behaving instinctively, and for them of course there is nothing indecent or immoral in the action. This is more than can be said for those people who, exploiting for gain their fellow men's weaknesses, do the same thing on the public stage. Most animals seek privacy when the annual or biennial rutting season comes round. It is only dogs who perform in public—often because they have no private place to retire to. Incidentally they are the only animals, apart from man, with sexual urges which operate outside the seasons laid down by nature—perhaps the result of two thousand years of life with man.

Such feelings as hatred, envy, covetousness and vindictive-ness are characteristic of human beings and unknown to animals. An animal's nature lacks such traits as falsehood, treachery and the lust for power; and it may well be this colossal difference between human beings and animals that makes it so difficult for the average man to understand the animal world.

Another barrier is the lack of communication between men and animals. It *is* possible to communicate with the animal world, but it takes so much effort and understanding that few people can summon up the mental energy even to make the attempt.

All living creatures have powers of telepathy, although in most people they remain latent and undeveloped. We are able to express ourselves in speech and writing, so that we no longer need to probe our neighbours' brains with the help of these telepathic powers. But it would have been better for us had we learned to master this innate ability. Most animals, on the other hand, have developed it to a high degree, and it is their most important means of communication.

Most animals can, to a greater or lesser extent, read people's thoughts. They cannot, of course, understand word for word what people are thinking, but they can appraise the feelings which these thoughts represent—hatred, falsehood, sympathy, affection. There are certain feelings which animals and human beings have in common, such as love, sympathy, pain, grief, and the maternal instinct. Animals are capable of recognizing all these in men; they are equally quick to recognize fear, antipathy, hatred and falsehood.

A dog or a cat—or for that matter any animal that has grown up among human beings—can learn to understand certain words which are in daily use, and which it associates with certain actions or events, especially those that affect its own well-being. But it is not primarily words that tell a dog what his master is trying to express: it is telepathy—and it operates with very few mistakes.

You should be very much on your guard against anybody whom your dog or cat regards with suspicion and antipathy. Soft words, good manners and a broad smile cut no ice with a dog. It can see through the mask and into the soul. I have never yet known an intelligent dog to misjudge anyone's character.

So far I have been talking of animals with a normal development and a well-balanced mentality. Unfortunately there are animals whose normal development has been interrupted—especially animals who have grown up with human beings, and above all, dogs. To satisfy our vanity and serve our own interests, we have bred dogs in a way that is totally contrary to nature. The result of inbreeding, and of certain kinds of cross-breeding, has been that many dogs today are mere caricatures of their ancestors, mentally as well as physically. Life in an increasingly neurotic society

has done the rest, so that today we can justly describe some dogs as neurotic.

Nerve clinics for dogs in need of psychiatric treatment are now commonplace in the more enlightened countries. The average man would do away with a dog that went off the rails; but there are people today who try to understand, and find another solution to his problem. A little psychology is often all that is needed.

A full-grown dog who suddenly, and for no apparent reason, starts urinating over the furniture is not being dirty or churlish. There is a very definite reason for his behaviour, and the reason can usually be traced back to the owner. To lead a normal, balanced life a man needs the security of a roof over his head and a bed to sleep in. The same is true of a dog. The home he lives in is *his* home—an absolutely vital part of his existence. If he loses his sense of belonging and feels he is living on alien territory by mere grace and favour—he loses his sense of security. His instinct for self-preservation suggests only two possible courses of action: to leave this 'home' for ever, or to mark it with his stamp of ownership. Instinctively he resorts to the primitive method employed out of doors by all animals for the purpose of informing the world that 'this belongs to me': he lifts a leg and sprinkles a little urine here and there. It is no use trying to thrash this out of the dog: he would die sooner than give up. The only solution is to give him what he is searching for: understanding and the sense of belonging to the family and the home.

This is just one example, but there is almost invariably a reason for a dog's behaviour in any circumstances. By making a determined effort to understand him, one usually finds that the explanation is quite simple.

The close relationship between a dog and his lord and master means that his character is strongly influenced by his master's. He watches him at every opportunity, trying to discover his thoughts, feelings and wishes, so that he can behave as he thinks his master wants him to. Thus by observing a dog we can often learn a lot about his owner. An aggressive dog often has a temperamental and aggressive owner. A nervous, cringing dog often comes from a home where there is little security or harmony.

I once met a man who had developed his powers of telepathy to such perfection that he could sit and converse intelligently with animals. I have been present at dozens of 'interviews' he conducted with animals who had problems, and I was impressed by the clarity of thought and capacity for understanding that are found in the animal brain.

We humans make the mistake of regarding animals as inferior beings, or even as insignificant objects. We should understand clearly that animals, like human beings, have a brain to think with and a heart that feels. They also possess a soul, which can be exalted or injured by their environment. There is no animal which does not far exceed mankind in loyalty, dignity and pride. If we can remember this we are a long way towards a deeper communion with nature—and life has few greater rewards to offer than the trust of the animal world.